REJOICE

into

JOY

BILL & BENI
JOHNSON

REJOICE
— *into* —
JOY

THREE KEYS TO EXPERIENCING THE
FULLNESS OF HEAVEN'S JOY

DESTINY IMAGE® PUBLISHERS, INC.
P.O. Box 310, Shippensburg, PA 17257-0310
"Promoting Inspired Lives."

This book and all other Destiny Image and Destiny Image Fiction books are available at Christian bookstores and distributors worldwide.

Cover design by Christian Rafetto

For more information on foreign distributors, call 717-532-3040.

Reach us on the Internet: www.destinyimage.com.

ISBN 13 TP: 978-0-7684-5740-7

ISBN 13 eBook: 978-0-7684-5741-4

For Worldwide Distribution, Printed in the U.S.A.

1 2 3 4 5 6 7 8 / 25 24 23 22 21

Rejoice in the Lord always [delight, take pleasure in Him]; again I will say, rejoice!

—Philippians 4:4 AMP

I will sing and greatly rejoice in Yahweh! My whole being vibrates with shouts of joy in my God! For he has dressed me with salvation and wrapped me in the robe of his righteousness! I appear like a bridegroom on his wedding day, decked out with a beautiful sash, or like a radiant bride adorned with sparkling jewels.

—Isaiah 61:10 TPT

CONTENTS

IN PURSUIT
OF JOY

Why is it right to sing, shout, dance, and leap? Why does God seem to want these radical expressions more than silent, awed reverence? While there is certainly a time for the latter, acts of *celebration* get way more press in the psalmist's descriptions of how we approach God. The reason—God is a God to celebrate. All His actions and thoughts toward us are extravagant expressions of His love, kindness, goodness, and delight in us; He gives it all not only to bless us for a moment, but to invite us into the deeper blessing of knowing Him.

He delights in us, so He wants us to delight in Him. He rejoices over us with singing (see Zeph. 3:17), so

He wants us to rejoice in Him with singing. When we give to Him what He gives to us, we step further into relationship with Him, deepening our heart connection with the source of life.

Not only that, but when we do what He is doing, aligning our bodies as well as our spirits and souls with what He has said, there is a release of His nature that flows to us in that place of intimacy. The Holy Spirit is the most joyful Person in existence, and joy is one of the primary expressions of His Kingdom in our lives (see Rom. 14:17). His command to "rejoice always" is really an expression of His desire for us to have joy! He is simply telling us how to receive it. We not only rejoice *because* we have joy—we rejoice in our *pursuit* of joy.

AN EXPRESSION
OF FAITH

I t certainly requires faith to rejoice when that's the last
thing you feel like doing or seems to make sense in
the face of your present circumstances. It doesn't take
much faith to hang your head and sing "Thou Art Worthy" when you're really just thinking, "I am worthless!"

Truly rejoicing in Him requires that you stand on
the truth that you are already accepted by Him where
you are. Rejoicing requires you to acknowledge that
His goodness and faithfulness are more real than your
present difficulty. It especially requires you to agree that
your life is not really about you!

Only the rejoicing that requires you to agree with
God's perspective on your situation is the sacrifice of

praise that pleases Him and has the power to transform you. It is the expression of faith. Sometimes that rejoicing is what David describes in Psalm 2:11: *"rejoice with trembling."* In other words, you don't have to feel full of faith to rejoice—you just have to do it.

THANKSGIVING, PRAISE, WORSHIP

While the natures of praise and thanksgiving are different, they should always go together, because they are sequential steps toward strengthening ourselves in His manifest presence. Psalm 100:4 says we *"enter into His gates with thanksgiving, and into His courts with praise."* This verse is a road map into the presence of God. Thus, our goal should be to sustain thanks and praise until our whole being is alive to His presence. But we also have to remember in that moment that the focus doesn't change from ministering to God to our getting what we need.

Thanksgiving and praise are tools to strengthen ourselves, not because they help us get something from the Lord but because they reconnect us to our primary purpose—to minister to Him in worship. They bring us into His presence, and true worship is something that only happens in that place of communion with His presence. In worship, the sacrifice is no longer physical expression or verbal declarations. We *are* the sacrifice. Fire always falls on sacrifice. And when we are the sacrifice, we cannot help but be changed.

THANKSGIVING

Give thanks to the Lord, for he is good! His faithful love endures forever.

—1 Chronicles 16:34 NLT

Whatever you do [no matter what it is] in word or deed, do everything in the name of the Lord Jesus [and in dependence on Him], giving thanks to God the Father through Him.

—Colossians 3:17 AMP

*From them will proceed thanksgiving
And the voice of those who celebrate;
And I will multiply them and they will not be
diminished; I will also honor them and they
will not be insignificant.*

—Jeremiah 30:19 NASB

THE WILL OF GOD

We are God's delegated authority. As such, our obedience plays an important role in seeing the will of God accomplished on the earth. In First Thessalonians 5:16-18, Paul instructs us to, *"Rejoice always, pray without ceasing, in everything give thanks; for this is the will of God in Christ Jesus for you."* Two things in this statement stand out.

First of all, the will of God is not merely focused on whether we become a doctor or a teacher or whether we're supposed to have tuna or peanut butter for lunch. It is focused on what we do to position our heart in relationship to God at all times, in all circumstances.

Second, rejoicing, prayer, and thanksgiving are all acts of *our* will that require faith, particularly in times of difficulty, weakness, and uncertainty. They are activities that draw our focus to Heaven so we can agree with what is true, no matter what we feel or perceive with our physical senses and emotions. And since our agreement is what attracts the strength and reality of Heaven into our lives and circumstances, it makes sense that these activities fulfill the will of God expressed in the Lord's Prayer—*on earth as it is in Heaven*. The transformation of the heart is the first step in bringing Heaven to earth.

Because rejoicing, prayer, and thanksgiving attract Heaven, they are vital tools for strengthening ourselves in the Lord. You'll notice that all of them are meant to be continuously ongoing in our lives. They're not reserved for crises or holidays. They're a lifestyle—as are all the tools that we use to minister to ourselves. A big reason for this is that in the midst of crisis and difficulty, it is usually hard if not impossible to sit down and reason out how we should respond. Difficulty has a way of exposing the degree to which our lives and minds have been truly transformed by a heavenly perspective for certain responses to be habitual. The things we practice as a lifestyle equip us for difficulties.

HONORING OUR RELATIONSHIP

Thankfulness carries an attitude of humility. Thanksgiving is the only proper way to receive what God has given us because it honors our relationship with Him by expressing trust in His goodness, even if we don't yet understand what we've received.

God gives us "every good and perfect gift" for two primary reasons (see James 1:17). He gives to make us prosper so we can succeed in life, and He gives to demonstrate His love as an invitation to relationship. When we practice thanksgiving as a lifestyle, we recognize that the gifts we have received from the Lord came with these purposes. Thanksgiving sets us on a course to know God in relation ship and discover the reasons for which He made us.

WITHHOLDING
THANKS

W hen God tells us to give Him thanks, He's not insinuating that He gives in order to get something from us. He doesn't manipulate us with His gifts. He wants us to thank Him because thankfulness acknowledges the truth about our lives. And when we agree with the truth, then the truth sets us free to see and manifest the greatness that He has put in us as the ones He has made in His image. When we withhold thanks from God, we actually cut ourselves off from who we are. This is what Paul explains in Romans 1:18-21:

> *For the wrath of God is revealed from heaven against all ungodliness and unrighteousness of*

*men, who suppress the truth in unrighteousness...
so that they are without excuse, because,
although they knew God, they did not glorify
Him as God, nor were thankful, but became
futile in their thoughts, and their foolish hearts
were darkened.*

Paul is basically saying that God has not kept who He is a secret. Knowing God is not hard. It's actually the most obvious thing in the world. All you have to do is glorify Him as God and be thankful. This response, because it agrees with the truth, gives you open access to the vast treasures of the knowledge of God. But without that response, your thoughts become *futile* and your heart is *darkened*.

Futile means "purposeless." When we fail to sustain the response of thanksgiving for everything in our lives, our thinking is cut off from our purpose in God. When we lose sight of our purpose, we will inevitably make choices that are outside of God's intentions for our lives, and this can only be destructive because it works against His design for us.

A dark heart is a heart that is unable to perceive spiritual reality. It is unmoved by the desires and affections of the Lord, and therefore cannot respond to His invitation to relationship, which is the source of life. As Paul goes on to explain in Romans chapter 1, a dark heart perverts our desires and leads us into all kinds of sin that degrades our identity and relationships. The most perverted sins known to mankind came about through a door left open because of the absence of thankfulness.

THANKSGIVING SANCTIFIES

S ince thanksgiving keeps us sane and alive by con-
necting us to the source of our life and purpose, it
makes sense that Paul instructs us to give thanks
"in everything" (see 1 Thess. 5:18). Thanksgiving keeps
us sane and alive. But there is a specific dimension of
thanksgiving that is particularly powerful in times of
difficulty and adversity. We find this principle in Paul's
first letter to Timothy:

> *Now the Spirit expressly says that in latter times
> some will depart from the faith, giving heed
> to deceiving spirits and doctrines of demons...
> commanding to abstain from foods which
> God created to be received with thanksgiving*

*by those who believe and know the truth. For
every creature of God is good, and nothing is to
be refused if it is received with thanksgiving; for
it is sanctified by the word of God and prayer.*
(1 Timothy 4:1-5)

Food was one of the biggest "disputable matters" that the early Church struggled with, particularly regarding the issue of eating food offered to idols. Jewish and Gentile believers alike feared that this food was defiled by having been dedicated to demonic spirits. False teachers of the time preyed upon this superstition and caused all kinds of bondage and division.

Interestingly, in this passage Paul doesn't debunk the superstition and say that dedicating food to idols is powerless. He simply says that combining thanksgiving with the Word and prayer is powerful enough to deauthorize that dedication and create a stronger one—a dedication to the Lord. He is saying thanksgiving *sanctifies* whatever it touches.

PARTICIPANTS
IN VICTORY

P salm 50 says, "*He who offers a sacrifice of thanks-giving honors Me; and to him who orders his way aright I shall show the salvation of God*" (Ps. 50:23 NASB). This is such a powerful verse. We have been made "*a royal priesthood*" (1 Pet. 2:9). As believers under the New Covenant, we now have the privilege of ministering to the Lord. When we offer up a "*sacrifice of praise,*" we are bringing honor to God.

Focusing our hearts on gratitude brings Him glory, which alone is enough. But the Bible goes on to explain that gratitude also reorients us correctly, inviting the "*salvation of God*" into our lives. That word *salvation* is the Hebrew word *yesha*, which means "rescue and safety," but it also means "deliverance, prosperity, and victory." The psalmist said to *enter His gates with thanksgiving and His courts with praise* (Ps. 100:4 NASB). When we come to the Lord with thankfulness, we have access to His presence and His covering. We get to participate in His victory.

REMEMBERING
THE COST

Jesus knew that Peter would deny Him, that His disciples would abandon Him, and that Judas was going to betray Him. But He still sat down to a meal with them and shared Communion. *"The Lord Jesus, on the night he was betrayed, took bread, and when he had given thanks, he broke it"* (1 Cor. 11:23-24 NIV). There are a few aspects here that teach me so much. He was well aware of the betrayal, yet Jesus still invited Judas to break bread with Him. He gave thanks.

Jesus filled His heart with gratitude, despite being aware that He was about to die and the very people He was dying for were betraying Him. I can't imagine the strength that Jesus had to have to walk through that moment the way that He did. Knowing that He was going to be crucified, He gave thanks. In the midst of betrayal, He opened His heart to His disciples.

There is a weight to remembering the cost that Jesus paid. I never want anyone to cultivate the heaviness that leads to depression. But there is an important humility and gravity that comes when you are remembering *how* His body was broken for us and *how* His blood was poured out for us. When I meditate on His experience, I remember all over again that His blood is sufficient for anything I am going through. Jesus paid the ultimate sacrifice so that I could be free and whole. If something is threatening that, I know it's not of the Lord. I can see what He went through to untangle me forever from sin and sickness.

RESPONDING IN GRATITUDE

Thankfulness is showing appreciation. The Bible tells us to *"Rejoice always; pray without ceasing; in everything give thanks; for this is God's will for you in Christ Jesus"* (1 Thess. 5:16-18 NASB). I often hear people yearning to know God's will for their lives, but it says it right here. Stay thankful. Stay connected to God.

When the Bible tells us to be thankful no matter the circumstance, it is not expecting us to create an emotion out of thin air. Gratitude is a response. There has to be a previous action or reality. When we take Communion, we are responding to all that the Lord has done and continues to do for us. Keeping our hearts postured toward the Lord in gratitude is one of the biggest keys to success we find throughout the Bible.

Hebrews 13:15 encourages us to "*continually offer up a sacrifice of praise to God*" (NASB). We've all been in the midst of experiences where the phrase "*sacrifice of praise*" feels very real. When you're exhausted or hurting, sometimes worship and expressing gratitude is the last thing you want to do. But look at the Samaritan leper.

Ten leprous men were healed by Jesus, but only one of them fell down to give Him thanks. Jesus wasn't in need of gratitude, but He knew that it would do something for the man. Jesus asked about the other nine men who hadn't returned, and then He told the Samaritan, "*Stand up and go; your faith has made you well*" (Luke 17:19 NASB). The man was already healed. But that word *well* is that Hebrew word *sozo* again. His body had been healed, but there was something about his expression of gratitude that made him whole.

UNACKNOWLEDGED GIFTS

Thanksgiving agrees with Heaven by acknowledging the truth that our lives are a gift from God and that He is sovereign over all. God is extravagantly generous, and the life He has given us to experience on this planet is not a life of survival but of abundance and blessing. But unless we properly recognize what we've been given, we won't be able to experience that life. That's the reality of receiving a gift. If we don't understand what we've been given, we won't understand its purpose and be able to experience its benefit.

Imagine Christmas morning. You've spent the last few months shopping and picking out unique gifts for each of your family members that show your intimate knowledge of their interests and desires. You have spared no expense to get gifts of the highest quality that will be both enjoyable and beneficial to each person. But when your family comes to the Christmas tree, one person completely ignores the presents. Another person opens your gift, but starts using it for something other than what it was made for. Still another just holds the gift, and refuses to unwrap it.

And to make matters worse, none of them even acknowledge that their gifts are from you. Can you see how these responses are not only foolish, but are deeply harmful to the relationship?

Sadly, this is how many Christians respond to God's gifts.

ACCOUNTABLE
FOR MIRACLES

We are accountable for what we've been given. It is up to us to keep the impact of an old experience current. I've seen people receive a dramatic touch from the Lord. And when they don't steward that touch, things go sour in their lives. Critics of revival tend to want to discount the touch of God and say, "See, I told you, that wasn't really God's touch on his life in the first place." Should God be questioned because of man?

Jesus talked about healing ten lepers. Only one returned to give thanks (see Luke 17:15-18). Does that mean that the other nine didn't really receive a touch from God? Of course not. The validity of God's work is never determined by man's response, good or bad. His work is measured by this: They had leprosy, and now they don't. Or, "I once was blind, but now I see" (see John 9:25). Or the person touched by God was healed of cancer. The doctor verified it. We give God all the praise.

THE GOD WHO INVADES
THE IMPOSSIBLE

As long as we steward our hearts before the Lord and allow His works to point us to Him, we will find that His works cannot fail to inspire awe, thanks, and celebration. And when I can be trusted to steward my heart in the seemingly simple things, I become qualified for the more critical. Keeping the testimony in our conversation also fills our hearts and minds with the revelation of God, creating a heightened awareness of His presence and His ways. This revelation trains our minds and hearts to perceive our circumstances from Heaven's perspective.

When I focus my attention on what God has done and is doing, I remain or become thankful. That one attitude of the heart changes my impact on the world around me, perhaps more than any other. It is that one characteristic that enables me to live aware of God.

Without a sustained awareness of the God who invades the impossible, I will reduce ministry to what I can accomplish with my ministry gifts. These gifts are like sails on a boat—without the wind, they're useless. We all need the wind of God to breathe on what we are gifted to do so that those gifts become eternally effective.

REMEMBERING
WHO GOD IS

If we fail to regularly *remember* who God is, what He has done, and what He is going to do, we *will* make decisions on the basis of what we can accomplish without Him, which restricts us to a life of the "possible." This leads to discouragement, small vision, mediocrity, burnout, and all the other problems that plague Christian leaders who lose touch with what God is doing.

For this reason, if I'm praying for someone with an injured joint, for example, and that person still has pain when she moves it, I don't allow myself to focus on that. I work to position myself to find out what God is doing in the situation and give Him thanks. I work to remember the testimony, because it helps me to build a case for healing, rather than building a case against it.

CULTIVATING GRATITUDE

That they should put their confidence in God and not forget the works of God, but keep His commandments.

(Psalm 78:7 NASB)

Dwelling on the goodness of God, continually reminding ourselves of His faithfulness and His promises—these are the building blocks of trust. And, when we trust God, aligning ourselves with His commandments comes so much more naturally. Without our keeping Him in the forefront of our minds, that confidence crumbles, and fear takes hold.

I love how *The Passion Translation* puts it in verse 22, talking about the Israelites who forgot God: "*They turned away from faith and walked away in fear; they failed to trust in his power to help them when he was near.*" There are very real consequences to our forgetting who God is. When His goodness and faithfulness are not fresh in our mind, we can become calloused toward God. We can feel hesitant to trust in His goodness. And that can lead to a heart that has not been cultivating gratitude.

We can see the results of that within our own lives and the lives of the Israelites. As soon as they started forgetting, they began to fear, and they put their trust in something else. Later, the same psalm speaks of the Lord's reaction to their unfaithfulness. "*He abandoned the dwelling place at Shiloh…and gave up His strength to captivity and His glory into the hand of the adversary*" (Ps. 78:60-61 NASB). This verse is incredibly sobering. Because of the Israelites' forgetfulness, because they turned from trusting in God completely, He allowed His presence to be removed from their midst. They were no longer recipients of His strength, and they no longer had access to His glory.

DO THE MATH

When I stay close to the presence of God through thanksgiving, I not only become aware of His absolute ability to invade the impossible, I sense His radical love and delight in me! As I give thanks for the good gifts He's put in my life, I present convincing evidence that He is my Father, He is for me, and His opinion pretty much cancels out all the others. The wonderful thing is that when we simply begin to give thanks, even when it seems difficult to remember one answered prayer, it isn't too long before our *focus* on the good in our lives creates an opening for the Lord's joy. And it's the joy of the Lord that is our strength.

I believe that James was talking about giving thanks when he said to *count* it all joy in trial, because giving thanks usually includes taking an inventory of God's gifts in your life. Do the math! If you want to discover the ability of thankfulness to bring you strength in difficulty, you need to keep *counting* these things *until* you come to the conclusion—it's time to rejoice! It becomes really hard to stay depressed about your circumstances when you're filled with the awareness of the love and goodness of God that surrounds and infuses your life.

There is a level of life we can reach where we practice thanksgiving as a lifestyle—a place where we remember our answered prayers. When difficulty comes along, we have a huge inventory of blessings instantly accessible to bring us into His presence as well as the joy and delight He has over us. That is a reality far greater than any accusation, crisis, or conflict that could come our way. When we learn to live in this realm, nothing can deflect us from our purpose. We even make the enemy help us get it done. From Heaven's perspective, it is reasonable to give thanks "in everything"!

THE DARKEST MOMENT

In First Corinthians 11, Paul unwraps the insight given to him through an encounter with Jesus Himself. In verses 23 and 24, he says, *"For I received from the Lord that which I also delivered to you: that the Lord Jesus on the same night in which He was betrayed took bread; and when He had given thanks, He broke it and said, 'Take, eat.'"*

Please picture something powerful—the very night that Jesus was betrayed, He gave thanks. In the midst of the ultimate betrayal, He gave an offering of thanksgiving. He didn't just tell us to praise Him in hard times; He gave us the ultimate example to follow. In betrayal, He gave thanks.

Thankfulness is one of the most vital attributes within the reach of every person alive. If I could prayerfully lay hands on people and impart a thankful heart, without question, I would. And I would make that the single greatest focus of my life. An impartation of thankfulness would have the greatest impact on the hearts and minds of people. It would literally change the world as we know it. Thankful people attract breakthrough.

Following the major sporting events like the Super Bowl, World Series, World Cup, and the like, it has become common to see athletes thank God for enabling them to win. I love to see them boast in God and testify of Him every chance they get. But let's be honest, it's not that challenging to give thanks when you've won.

The real prize is when we give Him thanks in the middle of something difficult or wrong. That's where the pearl is formed, so to speak. Pearls are formed through irritation. Whenever we give thanks in the middle of hard things, we are presenting something to Him that is priceless. Jesus did it at His darkest moment—betrayal.

WORTHY OF OUR TRUST

The apostle Paul faced some of the most extreme experiences that one could face. And it was from prison he wrote some of the most helpful insights for our lives:

> *Rejoice in the Lord always; again I will say, rejoice! ...Be anxious for nothing, but in everything by prayer and supplication with thanksgiving let your requests be made known to God. And the peace of God, which surpasses all comprehension, will guard your hearts and your minds in Christ Jesus.*
>
> (Philippians 4:4-7 NASB)

Rejoicing, prayer, supplication, and thanksgiving all help to settle the battle for our minds. In the verse that follows, Paul gives us insight on what to fill our minds with (see Phil. 4:8). The implication is that if it is filled with the things of God, there will be no room for thoughts that violate our view of His nature. And whenever we discover His nature, we also discover our new nature in Christ. We always become like the One we trust.

It is important to pray, bringing our needs, fears, and challenges to God. He welcomes us in any state we are in. But the prayers of authority are never prayed in fear. Fear-based prayers are the prayers of servants, not sons and daughters. Again, He welcomes me in whatever condition I am in. In His mercy, He ministers to us and heals us. But He has called us into a lifestyle that is much higher than that.

I encourage people to pray until the fear and anxiety are gone. For me this process always involves worship and feeding my heart on the promises of God. As we return to a place of faith, we become useful co-laborers in making the decrees necessary to bring about God's will in a given situation. Giving thanks is what helps to keep us in tune with our Father who never lies and is always worthy of our trust. Thankfulness flows effortlessly from the one who has experienced this internal victory.

FOCUSING
ON THE KING

We don't wage warfare in the Kingdom by focusing on the devil. We keep our focus on the King and His Kingdom, and the devil cannot help but be unseated by God's ever-increasing government released through our lives, which illustrates another reason why thanksgiving is powerful in times of adversity. Psalm 100:4 says that we *"enter into His gates with thanksgiving."*

Thanksgiving brings us into the manifest presence of God and connects us with what He is doing and saying in the midst of our circumstances. Thanksgiving helps to establish our focus on Him so that our awareness shifts from earthly reality to heavenly reality—which we must do in order to release the strength of Heaven into our circumstances.

I have purposed to try to live in such a way that nothing ever gets bigger than my consciousness of God's presence. Sometimes conflict can be as simple as bad news on TV. If it starts to weigh on my heart and grow bigger than my awareness of God, I consciously turn my affection toward Him to become more aware of His presence. If that doesn't work, I turn off the TV or leave the room to redirect my focus until my awareness of Him is bigger than that which weighs heavily on my heart.

I can't just know in my head that He's bigger; I have to have my entire being in a position where I am aware of His presence and expect His world to invade my life and circumstances. If I don't sustain this expectation, I will expect other forces to be the prime movers in my life and will begin to live defensively instead of offensively.

GREAT WITH
GRATITUDE

There is a great story where Elijah is praying for rain. He puts his head between his knees and cries out to God. Elijah's servant goes up on the hill and then comes back, saying, "I don't see anything. There's no sign of rain at all." Finally, the last time he comes down, he says, "I do see a cloud the size of a man's hand" (see 1 Kings 18:42-44).

That is not a cloud to be impressed with, but Elijah knew it was the beginning. He ran for cover because he knew small beginnings explode into great expressions when we respond in faith. Jesus did something very similar. He took bread and He broke it and gave thanks for it, and then it was multiplied (see Luke 9:16). It's an unusual but amazing illustration that small things can become great with gratitude. Increase and greatness are brought about when we steward the portion that He has given to us.

MAINTAINING AWE

Testimonies keep us encouraged and aware. It is simply impossible to sit through an extended time of hearing how Heaven has been invading earth all over our city and the world and go away discouraged. When we share these stories with one another, we are releasing the anointing of the spirit of prophecy over one another, saying, "This is our God. This is what He's like. This is what He's doing, and this is what He's going to do." It gives us grace to face whatever impossibilities we are currently facing.

Sadly, it is possible to lose a sense of awe and gratitude for the miraculous. It is almost hard to imagine, but Israel grumbled frequently to God in the wilderness in spite of the fact that every day for 40 years they experienced divine health, manna on the ground, and shoes that didn't wear out—plus the visible sign of God's presence among them with the cloud and pillar of fire.

We are in danger of this same complacency when we don't cultivate a heart of thankfulness and expectation. If we are unimpressed with miracles, it is a warning sign that we are allowing bitterness, unbelief, or the hardening of our hearts toward God. Or we have simply stopped being thankful for what God is doing and allowed ourselves to set our hearts on what He isn't doing.

SET APART FOR
HIS PURPOSE

Giving thanks for something sets it apart for God and His purposes. It changes it into something holy. This extends to every situation in your life in which you find other powers at work besides the power of God. It's vital to remember that not everything that happens in life is His will. He didn't cause the crisis a nation or individual may be facing. He actually can't give things that are not good because He doesn't have them.

Someone can only give what he has. God only gives good gifts, because He is good, and has only good gifts to give. So giving thanks in everything does not mean saying that the adversity came from God. But giving thanks in the midst of an adverse situation, a difficulty intended to undermine your faith and destroy you, enables you to take hold of that situation and set it apart to God and His purposes.

When you give thanks, the weapon the enemy meant to use to dislodge you from your divine purpose is put into your hands and becomes the very thing that brings you more fully into that purpose. Jesus declared that He sends us out with the same assignment the Father gave to Him—to destroy the works of the devil (see 1 John 3:8). Thanksgiving accomplishes the divine justice of the Kingdom, where the enemy is destroyed by the very thing he intended to use for our destruction. Just knowing that we can participate in destroying the enemy's purposes should alone move us to give thanks!

A QUIET AND TRANQUIL LIFE

When the apostle Paul taught Timothy about God's will for people's daily lives, he got really practical. He started with a prayer direction, but then transitioned into revealing the wonderful outcome of the prayer direction. This is found in First Timothy 2:1-4:

> *First of all, then, I urge that entreaties and prayers, petitions and thanksgivings, be made on behalf of all men, for kings and all who are in authority, so that we may lead a tranquil and quiet life in all godliness and dignity. This is good and acceptable in the sight of God our*

Savior, who desires all men to be saved and to come to the knowledge of the truth (NASB).

The direction for our lives is simple but important. Pray for all in authority, with thankfulness. It is usually fairly easy to pray for those in authority, but it's not always easy to be thankful for them. When we consider that Paul lived at a time of extremely abusive leaders, we realize that this was not an untested theory or a flowery suggestion. His insight has teeth to it because of his own experience. Cultivating a heart that values leaders regardless of how little godliness is in their lives is a challenge, but with great reward. Being thankful for them before they deserve it qualifies them for a visitation of God in a most remarkable way.

God's will is a *tranquil and quiet life*. Tranquil means *free from disturbance*. And quiet means *uninterrupted*. That is the heart of God for every city on earth—that His purpose for our well-being would be without disturbance and interruption. That alone should appeal to everyone. In that atmosphere, there is a future and a hope. What a profound outcome for those praying for their leaders with thankfulness.

PRAISE

And those who know Your name will put their
trust in You; For You, Lord, have not forsaken
those who seek You. Sing praises to the Lord,
who dwells in Zion! Declare His
deeds among the people.

—Psalm 9:10-11

Yours, O Lord, is the greatness, the power, the
glory, the victory, and the majesty. Everything
in the heavens and on earth is yours, O Lord,
and this is your kingdom. We adore you
as the one who is over all things.

—1 Chronicles 29:11 NLT

*All praises belong to the God and Father of
our Lord Jesus Christ. For he is the Father of
tender mercy and the God of endless comfort.*

—2 Corinthians 1:3 TPT

*You who fear the Lord, praise him! All you
descendants of Jacob, honor him! Revere him,
all you descendants of Israel!*

—Psalm 22:23 NIV

A LIFESTYLE
OF PRAISE

Thanksgiving should naturally lead to rejoicing when we follow James' instruction to "*count it all joy.*" As we count up all that God has done, we shouldn't stop at merely thanking God. In every one of the acts of God is a revelation of His nature. And as we see God's nature—His extravagance, joy, love, faithfulness, goodness, and power—the only sensible response is to praise Him. Praise and rejoicing are two sides of the same coin, as we see in Psalm 9:2: "*I will be glad and rejoice in You; I will sing praise to Your name, O Most High.*"

It's hard to praise effectively without rejoicing, without bringing our body, soul, and spirit into an expression of celebration. We can't rejoice without having a reason, and that reason is God's nature, revealed in His relationship with us, that we declare in our praises. When God says to "*rejoice always*," the implication is that we are to establish praise as a lifestyle.

The praise that flows from thanksgiving is described in Hebrews 13:15 as a "sacrifice." This verse gives us a guideline for what kinds of activities genuinely qualify as praise. First of all, praise should cost us something. Only then is it a proper response to the God who has given us the costly gift of His own Son.

When I force myself to rejoice, I am offering God my time, my focus, and my comfort. I am stepping beyond what is convenient and beyond all the pressures of my circumstances. That is what makes the act of praise a costly expression. Second, a sacrifice of praise should always require faith because it's impossible to please Him apart from faith. Hebrews 11:4 explains that it was "*By faith Abel offered to God a more excellent sacrifice than Cain.*"

PHYSICAL
OBEDIENCE

The only way to break an agreement with a lie is *repentance*, which means to change the way you think. In that place of praise, I feed my mind on the truth of God's nature *until* it creates a new agreement with heavenly reality. When that agreement is established, the reality starts to manifest in my emotions, mind, and body. Making an agreement with Heaven actually requires more than repentance of the mind.

You need physical proof to make repentance a legally binding reality. By lining my physical body up with what the Word said, I brought my whole being into agreement with the truth. In doing so, I experienced the principle that physical obedience brings spiritual breakthrough.

This may seem a little backward to those of us who hate the idea of going through religious motions and desire to be "authentic" in our worship.

Physical obedience brings spiritual breakthrough. But the measure of authenticity is not what you're feeling or thinking. Those things either line up with authentic reality or they don't. And if they don't, Scripture tells us that we get there by *moving*. Some say it's hypocritical to do something you don't feel like doing. I think it's hypocritical to do only what I feel like doing and call myself a believing believer. Right actions release right emotions and right thinking.

DANCING BEFORE
THE PRESENCE

avid announced the new plan to usher God's presence into his city. The people were ready. The priests were ready. The priestly musicians trained for the day. Those assigned to carry the ark of His presence probably wondered about the fearfully exciting privilege involved in their job. After all, the last guy to get that close to the Ark died. But this time they had the will of God revealed in Scripture to support the process.

This story is one of the greatest stories in the Bible. It should be known forward and backward by every believer, as it is key to clearly fulfilling our role in this day. It is our story, ahead of time.

The day came. King David stripped himself of his kingly garments and put on a priest's tunic, basically a priest's undergarment. This was not something a king would be seen in normally. But then David was not a normal king. He would become known as the man after God's heart—the man of God's presence. After six steps, they stopped and sacrificed an ox to the Lord. He then danced before the Ark with all of his might.

This must have been a fearfully beautiful sight. All of Israel was lining the streets, rejoicing in the actual presence of God. The musicians played with great skillfulness. As much as it was possible, a nation showed up for an event. The grandeur, the magnificence and sheer volume must have been overwhelming. Everyone present was impacted by this *once in a lifetime* experience.

It is worth noting that the Ark of the Covenant (the presence of God) followed David into Jerusalem. Wherever David danced, God followed. He responds to our offerings. In this story, it's an offering of thanksgiving and praise expressed in the dance. Many respond to God once His presence is realized. But some respond before

He actually comes. They are the ones who usher in the presence of the King of Glory. Another way of looking at it is God showed up wherever King David danced in an undignified fashion. It might surprise us to find out what is attractive to Him.

RESPONDING
TO PRAISE

As God's presence becomes manifest upon a worshiping people, even unbelievers are brought into an encounter with God. My son and daughter have ministered to the Lord on troubled streets in San Francisco. As people walked by, we saw many who manifested demons while others broke out in joyful laughter as they came into the presence of the Lord.

These things shouldn't surprise us. Look at how God responds to the praises of His people as mentioned in Isaiah 42:13: *"The Lord shall go forth like a mighty man; He shall stir up His zeal like a man of war. He shall cry out, yes, shout aloud; He shall prevail against His enemies."*

INHABITING OUR PRAISE

Jesus taught us to pray, "*Our Father in heaven, hallowed be Your name*" (Matt. 6:9). The title *Father* is a title of honor and a call to relationship. What He did to make it possible for us to call Him "our Father" is all one needs to see to begin to become a true worshiper. "Hallowed" means respected or revered. This too is an expression of praise. In the book of Revelation, which is actually entitled The Revelation of Jesus Christ (not the antichrist!) (see Rev. 1:1), it is obvious that praise and worship are the primary activities of heaven. And so it is to be for the believer here on earth. The more we live as citizens of heaven, the more heaven's activities infect our lifestyles.

Worship is our number-one priority in ministry. Everything else we do is to be affected by our devotion to this call. He inhabits our praise. One translation puts it this way, *"But You are holy, enthroned in the praises of Israel"* (Ps. 22:3). God responds with a literal invasion of heaven to earth through the worship of the believer.

CAUGHT UP
IN HIS NATURE

I want to be used by God as much as anybody I know. I love when He uses me to bring a miracle to somebody's body or their mind or to lead someone to Christ. It is such a joy to be used to bring deliverance from the torment that the enemy often brings to people's lives. These are such wonderful opportunities. But what I don't want to do is fall into the trap of developing an intimacy with God so that He will use me.

I want to learn to hear His voice not so that He'll use me, but so that I can interact with Him. Of course, He is going to use me, but the focus is relationship. I don't ever want to use my relationship with Him so that I can reach a spiritual goal. I want to know Him. In knowing Him, I have the privilege of making Him known.

I want to know His heart. I want to know His ways, not so that I can put another notch on my Bible that another case of cancer was healed, but because I want to display who He is. I want to be trusted by Him as a son who will represent Him well when He speaks and be silent when He doesn't. I want to know His ways because I'm caught up with His nature and who He is.

HIS WORKS BRING HIM PRAISE

*Now when the multitudes saw it, they marveled
and glorified God, who had given such power
to men.*

(Matthew 9:8)

I talk about the miracle-working power of God in almost every meeting I lead, whether it be a traditional church service, a conference, even a board or staff meeting. When I'm speaking away from home, I will often do this to stir up faith and help listeners to direct their hearts to God.

When I'm through, I ask them this question: *How many of you gave praise and glory to God when I shared those testimonies?* Most every hand goes up. Then I remind them of this one important thing—*if there were no power and corresponding testimony, God would have never received that glory. Without power, we rob God of the glory He is due!*

> *All Your works shall praise You, O Lord, and Your saints shall bless You.*
>
> (Psalm 145:10)

Not only do miracles stir the hearts of men to give glory to God, miracles give Him glory on their own. I'm not sure how this works, but somehow an act of God has a life of its own and contains the ability to actually give God glory without the assistance of mankind. The absence of miracles robs God of the glory that He is to receive from the life released in His own works.

SPIRITUAL INHERITANCE

Every generation has had to learn from scratch how to recognize the presence, how to move with Him, how to pay a price. The answer to this tragedy is inheritance, where you and I receive something for free. What we do with it determines what happens in the following generations. God is serious about returning for a glorious Church. He's serious that nations should serve Him—not just a token representation from every tribe and tongue, but entire nations, entire people groups apprehended by God Himself.

Can you imagine what would happen if entire nations stepped into the gifts they have from God? Where the song of praise, the declarations of God and

His greatness and goodness became visibly manifest on a people? That's His heart. But if we're to get there, we must understand and embrace our spiritual inheritance.

We were never intended to start over from scratch every two or three generations. God wants to put each generation at a higher level than the previous one. Every generation has a ceiling experience that becomes the next generation's floor. We dishonor our forefathers and the great price they paid to get their breakthrough by not maintaining and expanding what they accomplished. They attained by tremendous risk and persevering under ridicule and rejection. The things we take for granted today cost the previous generation tremendously.

GROWING
IN AFFECTION

During church, we have had times recently when cancer has simply disappeared in worship. We've had times when a person's eyesight has been completely healed in the presence of God. A man was visiting us from another country not too long ago, and he came to Bethel because so many people had been telling him to go. As he sat there during worship, he felt someone spill hot coffee down his back.

He turned, frustrated that someone would be so careless. But, as he turned around, he realized that there was no one there. Suddenly, he realized that a serious injury to his shoulder had been healed. God had manifested His presence through that fire that touched his back, and he was healed.

Miracles are happening increasingly like this. It is not because we have gotten smarter or have developed greater strategies, but because we are relational. We are growing in a deep affection for the Holy Spirit, and from that place we are learning how to host Him, giving Him first place. We are learning how to champion what He champions and withdraw from what He withdraws from. This is who we have been designed to be—a people born for the glory.

WEAPONS OF WAR

Beni teaches that Communion is a weapon of war, and I really believe that. This meal is not only an act of celebration but also a military tool of battle. We may not feel like we are engaging in war, but there are many things that we do—celebrating His kindness and His goodness, delighting in His presence, and giving praise—that all have a military effect on the demonic realm. Psalm 68:1 says, *"Let God arise, let His enemies be scattered."* When we exalt the Lord, there is an effect on the realms of darkness.

The Lord has given us basically four different weapons for spiritual warfare—the blood of Jesus (Communion), the Word of God, the name of Jesus, and praise. Those are the four basic weapons that we believers use in our life that defeat and overcome the assaults that the enemy brings against us. None of them are focused on the devil. All of them are focused on the provision of the Lord and the Person of the Lord Jesus Christ.

As a church, we're on a journey to learn how to access all that God has purchased for us. The blood of Jesus is the legal basis for all victory. The cross of Jesus was so thorough in its victory that everything you will ever need throughout eternity was purchased at this one event. There's no other event in history that was so all-inclusive. A hundred billion years from now we will still be feeding off of what was provided for in the sacrifice of this unblemished Lamb.

NATURAL BECOME SUPERNATURAL

We instinctively know that when we give money to help the poor, or to support our local church or another project for the Kingdom, the gift has a supernatural effect. That really is an amazing truth. The money we all hold in our hands has been used for so many things. Some of them good, like groceries, clothing, and food. But it has also been used for drugs, pornography, etc. And that money is now in my hands, and through generosity I can shape the course of history with it, as it will surely bring forth fruit for His glory.

The profound conclusion is that the natural becomes supernaturally effective through giving. But what would happen if we did the same with our family time, our work schedule, our fellowship, etc.? It's the same concept.

That which we gave to Him becomes supernaturally effective because it was placed into His hands as a gift. Our efforts that may seem so insignificant are very similar to the boy's lunch. It was enough to feed a child. But once it was placed in the Master's hands, it became supernaturally effective enough to feed a multitude. So is every offering we give to Him as we learn to worship in all areas of life.

OUR REASON
TO REJOICE

God certainly gave them yet another good reason to rejoice in Him with real joy. He is more than ready to convince us that He is worthy of our praise. But more than that, He is hoping we'll respond to His invitation to walk in a mature relationship with Him, one in which our primary focus, like His, is not on *getting* but *giving*.

Times of difficulty give us an opportunity we don't have otherwise, and that is the opportunity to demonstrate sacrificial love to Him by ministering to Him instead of attending to our pressing needs. In those times, we give Him praise solely because we are convinced that knowing Him is the reason to rejoice.

When He sees that singleness of heart for Him, that total abandonment, He can't stay away.

This kind of relationship is what makes strengthening yourself in the Lord completely opposed to self-sufficiency. It works according to the logic of the Kingdom, which says that you must lose your life to save it. You must give in order to receive. If you need strength, you give yourself so totally to the Lord and His purposes that the Lord becomes the only One who can give you the supernatural strength you need.

PRAISE AMIDST UNCERTAINTY

One of the toughest lessons a Christian can learn is how to trust and praise God in the uncertain time between a promise and its fulfillment. I believe it is a powerful act of spiritual warfare to stand in the middle of death and disease, conflict and unresolved issues, and to cause your spirit to rise and give thanks to God.

Why do we have to endure uncertainty? That is a mystery, but the Bible hints at an answer when it gives a spiritual picture of a city called the community of the redeemed, or Zion (see Isa. 62). Isaiah 60:18 says, *"But you shall call your walls Salvation, and your gates Praise."* In Revelation we see this gate called praise again and discover that is made out of one solid pearl (see Rev. 21:21). Think for a moment. How is a pearl formed? Through irritation and conflict. A granule of sand gets inside an oyster shell, and a pearl forms around the granule to keep it from doing harm.

The Bible's pairing of praise with irritation is not coincidental. When we are stuck in conflict and uncertainty, and yet we praise Him without manipulation, it is a sacrifice. It means we are reacting in a way that produces something beautiful. In that moment, a gate is formed, a place of entrance where the King of glory can invade our situation.

Many people have no gate because they won't praise Him in the middle of apparent paradox. They get stuck wondering, "How can God promise to heal all of my diseases but I've got this problem in my body?" "How can God promise to provide, and yet I've been without a job for three months?" And yet Psalm 87:2 says, "*The Lord loves the gates of Zion more than all the dwellings of Jacob.*" That gate—that place of praise in the midst of conflict—is where His presence rests, where the King

Himself dwells. The gate is formed when we move above human explanation and into a place of trust.

When you find yourself in an uncertain time—and you surely will at some point—remember that you can create a gate of praise by lifting your heart and your voice to God. Persistently pursue fellowship with God even though your uncertainty feels deep and endless, and no answers have materialized. The suffering will last but a moment in God's grand plan for your life. Be thankful for the opportunity to persevere. And be assured— better times are on the way!

PAYING
THE PRICE

Proverbs 13:22 says, *"A good man leaves an inheritance for his children's children."* Righteousness causes us to realize that our daily decisions affect several generations away. We must learn to sow into the welfare of a generation we may never live to see.

I think of my father, who was a great general in the army of God. What I and my church are experiencing right now is beyond what I used to dream. But much of it, if not all of it, is because my dad paid a price.

I watched him when I was a young man. I watched him push ahead as a forerunner, enduring so much criticism and rejection. He honorably displayed what it looked like to value the presence of God above the opinions and support of man. It cost him severely, but he left a rich inheritance for our family, as well as for the Church in our region.

In the final five days of his life, 20 or more family members were with my dad, singing praise and ministering to God, because that's what he taught us. He taught us that in all situations you give honor to God. It's our highest honor to bless His great Name and take delight in Him. He showed us how.

So we were with him hour after hour, worshiping, giving glory to God, praying, sharing testimonies, telling family stories, finding time to rest in shifts, and then singing once again. We did this 24 hours a day in a constant cycle. And then he died. And we wept. We did all the things grieving families do. We were so sorry for our loss, happy for his reward.

A FRAGRANT
SACRIFICE

While God is big enough to use every situation for His glory, it doesn't mean that the given problem was His will. Not everything that happens in life is God's will. We must stop blaming Him. The cornerstone of our theology is the fact that *God is always good and is the giver of only good gifts*. He is always faithful, and always keeps His promises. There is no evil or darkness in Him.

His goodness and faithfulness become the focus of my praise. I celebrate those aspects of His nature during what sometimes appear to be *contradictory circumstances*. After my dad's death, I discovered the privilege of giving God a sacrificial offering of praise that I will never be able to give Him in eternity. My offering was given in the midst of sadness, disappointment, and confusion—none of which will I ever experience in Heaven. Only in this life will we be able to give an offering with that kind of "fragrance."

PRAISING INTO BREAKTHROUGH

Praise isn't pleasing to the flesh, which may be one reason why it's so powerful in removing that cloud of oppression. The enemy is empowered by human agreement. To agree with anything he says gives him a place to kill, steal, and destroy. We fuel the cloud of oppression by agreeing with our enemy. Praise, with rejoicing, cancels that agreement.

Praise was one of the primary tools that God had equipped me with as a young man to strengthen myself in the discouragement of my early years as a pastor. I could be questioning a million things about my life, but I never had to question whether I was in the right place when I was giving God praise. It became my default when I slid into the fog of confusion and depression.

In Weaverville, our home was behind the church, so I often went to the sanctuary late at night, put worship music on the sound system, and spent time praising and worshiping God. Sometimes I remained until early in the morning. I danced, shouted, and basically required myself to do whatever I didn't *feel* like doing.

The psalmist David wrote, *"Bless the Lord, O my soul."* He commands his own soul to come into order and give God glory. It's important that we learn how to bring our souls and even our bodies into submission to the purposes of God. Back then I would make sure that the intensity of my praise was in equal proportion to the size of the cloud over my head. Every time, there would come a point when something inside of me would shift, and I was no longer making an effort. My mind, will, emotions, and body were completely filled with conviction of what I was declaring to the Lord. I also noticed that the cloud over my head had disappeared and I was alive in God!

I came to understand that the cloud wasn't just *over* my head; it was *inside* it. I mistakenly thought that focusing on my lack and comparing myself to others was a posture of humility. In fact, it was the opposite. Instead of focusing on God's greatness in my life, I was focusing on myself. I was actually agreeing with the enemy by making my own problems bigger than God's promises. And my agreement invited that cloud of oppression to hover over me.

CLEARING
THE WAY

One powerful concept in the Kingdom is that you get more of what you have by correctly stewarding what you have. If we can make that adjustment and learn to live in grace, our conduct changes so much more dramatically than when we try to work to obtain favor. Some of God's commands are not so much to require performance as to create correct appetites. Living out of passion is so much more Christ-like than merely living out of good discipline.

The prophet Isaiah continues with this beautiful picture of a highway for people:

> *Go through, go through the gates, clear the way for the people; build up, build up the*

highway, remove the stones, lift up a standard over the peoples.

(Isaiah 62:10 NASB)

I believe the gates in this passage refer to *praise,* as mentioned several verses earlier in Isaiah 60:18. When the people of God give God praise, something happens in the atmosphere. Praise in effect clears the way for people. The obstacles of impure ideologies, culture, and spiritual strongholds are confronted. Continuous praise that is both sacrificial and pure eventually removes all inferior realities, establishing a Heaven-like realm over geographical locations. It happens wherever the people of God gather to worship.

But when it is sustained and pure, it eventually has an effect on entire cities. This heavenly atmosphere changes people's perception of reality. This process is called *building a highway.* A worshiping community changes the atmosphere over the city that actually creates a realm of easy access to know Christ for those who don't know Him. There is a profound connection in the unseen realm between our praises, His glory, His goodness, and the great harvest of souls.

DESERVING
OUR PRAISE

The Holy Spirit is de-emphasized and almost removed from many Christians' daily approach to life and the Word. The fear of becoming like some mindless fanatic has kept many a Christian from interacting with their greatest treasure in this life—the Holy Spirit. We are heirs of God, and the Holy Spirit is the down payment of our inheritance (see Eph. 1:13-14).

Some teach that we shouldn't talk much about the Spirit as the Holy Spirit doesn't speak of Himself. However, both the Father and Son have a lot to say about Him. It is wise to listen to them. God is to be praised, adored, boasted in, and interacted with—and the Holy Spirit is God.

PRAISING GOD
WITH TONGUES

When God calls a particular baptism a *baptism of fire*, it is obviously not one of mere refreshing. Heaven has come to influence earth in this baptism. But when that rushing mighty wind came and the language of Heaven poured forth from their lips, they also were refreshed by what influenced them. Paul would later point out that praying in tongues edifies us.

There's little doubt about that happening to the small group of believers on the day of Pentecost. To top it off, they were speaking something so completely satisfying, so accurate and powerful, that it was like experiencing a completely new day. And they were. This heavenly language came as an eruption from their hearts. But for the first time in their lives, and actually in all of history, they said what needed to be said perfectly without missing it or falling short in one way or another.

The Spirit of God spoke through them with brilliant understanding of whom He was exalting. Their praise went right from the Spirit of God, through their yielded lips, to God Himself. In this instance, the human intellect was bypassed. They were *"speaking of the mighty deeds of God"* (Acts 2:11 NASB). This time, the language was a language of praise—not prayer.

Imagine the privilege it was to speak of the great mysteries of God's nature over a city that had rejected Him. It was intoxicating, to say the least. The intention of the Lord is that this baptism of fire would ignite every heart. This would be best expressed by a people who were presence-driven instead of ministry-driven. It's not about what I can accomplish for God. It's all about who goes with me and my doing all I can to protect that most valuable connection.

ENTHRONED
ON OUR PRAISES

Here are a just a couple of the promises in Scriptures regarding the benefits we receive when we're faithful to give Him praise and worship. Psalm 22:3 declares, *"You are holy, enthroned in the praises of Israel."* Our praises actually create a platform in our circumstances for the King to sit on His throne and release the reality of His Kingdom. And when the Kingdom comes, it always destroys the kingdom of darkness. This is how Isaiah describes it:

> *Sing to the Lord a new song, and His praise from the ends of the earth, you who go down to the sea, and all that is in it, you coastlands and you inhabitants of them! Let the wilderness*

and its cities lift up their voice, the villages that Kedar inhabits. Let the inhabitants of Sela sing, let them shout from the top of the mountains. Let them give glory to the Lord, and declare His praise in the coastlands. The Lord shall go forth like a mighty man; He shall stir up His zeal like a man of war. He shall cry out, yes, shout aloud; He shall prevail against His enemies.

(Isaiah 42:10-13)

He's basically saying that while Israel is celebrating and praising God, God is taking it upon Himself to go out and destroy their enemies. What a deal! This is what happens when God is enthroned in our praises.

ACTIVITIES
OF PRAISE

Every part of life is beautiful and has the potential to bring Him glory. Merely offering our efforts unto Him sanctifies that which was previously thought to be secular, vain, or mundane. I was able to see that every part of my life was sanctified by its eternal purpose.

So many think ministry is standing behind a pulpit and preaching. Thankfully, that is included, as that is a part of my assignment. But in reality, it is a very small part of that vast subject. This is important to understand. If we don't realize what our actions mean to God, we do not receive the strength and encouragement God intended for us out of our own obedience.

The moment all of us are waiting for is when He says, *"Well done, good and faithful servant"* (Matt. 25:23). I realize this is speaking of a future event. But He breathes that into our heart every time we know with confidence that we have done the will of God. Doing what brings Him pleasure—whether it's preaching, praying for the sick, or going on a picnic with my family—delights the heart of our Father who takes it personally.

It's the manner in which we do what we do. Laying hands on the sick, or working in the garden, or even going to a Little League game all become spiritual activities of praise because of who they are done for. Worship sanctifies the offering.

DECLARATIONS OF PRAISE

The Kingdom of God is His possession, which is why He alone can give it to us (see Luke 12:32). When we declare that reality, we move into declarations of praise! All through the Scriptures we hear the declarations of praise similar to this one contained in His model prayer declaring that *all glory and power* belong to Him.

One of the most important teachings that I have ever received came from Derek Prince about 30 years ago. It was a wonderful message on praise. In it, he suggested that if we only have ten minutes to pray, we should spend about eight praising God. It's amazing how much we can pray for with the two minutes we have left.

That illustration helped me to reinforce the priority of worship that I was learning from my pastor—my dad.

Once again, the prayer Jesus taught us to pray in the book of Matthew has two main objectives: 1) minister to God out of an intimate personal relationship; and 2) bring the reality of His rulership (the Kingdom) to earth. The Kingdom approach to prayer reveals to us a prayer for heaven to invade our material needs, our personal relationships, and our own relationship to evil. But that request is sandwiched between praise and worship for who God is.

PRAISE DESTROYS THE POWERS OF HELL

I was not left on planet earth to be in hiding, waiting for Jesus' return. I am here as a military representative of heaven. The Church is on the attack; that's why "*the gates of Hades,*" the place of demonic government and strength, "*shall not prevail*" against the Church (Matt. 16:18).

> *He increased His people greatly, and made them stronger than their enemies. He turned their heart to hate His people, to deal craftily with His servants.*
>
> (Psalm 105:24-25)

First, God makes us strong, and then He stirs up the devil's hatred toward us. Why? It's not because He wants to create problems for His Church. It's because He likes to see the devil defeated by those who are made in His image, who have a relationship of love with Him by choice. We are His delegated authority. It is His delight to have us enforce the triumph of Jesus. "*To execute on them the written judgment—this honor have all His saints*" (Ps. 149:9).

> *Let the inhabitants of Sela sing aloud. ...He will arouse His zeal like a man of war. He will utter a shout, yes, He will raise a war cry. He will prevail against His enemies.*
> (Isaiah 42:11,13 NASB)

Our ministry to God is one of life's most important privileges. Praise honors God. But it also edifies us and destroys the powers of hell! It's amazing to think that I can praise Him, have His peace fill my soul, and have Him say that I am a mighty man of valor. All I did was praise Him. He destroyed the powers of hell on my behalf and gave me the "points" for the victory.

AN ATMOSPHERIC
SHIFT

We know that He inhabits our praise (see Ps. 22:3). It stands to reason that presence is released. Atmosphere is changed. In fact, the atmosphere of Jerusalem came about in part because of worship. *"We hear them in our own tongues speaking of the mighty deeds of God"* (Acts 2:11 NASB). Such praise contributed to an atmospheric shift over an entire city where the spiritual blindness was lifted, followed by 3,000 souls being saved.

I've seen this myself when we've rented a particular facility for church services, only to have the people who use it afterward comment on the presence that remains. A friend of mine used to take people onto the streets in San Francisco many years ago. They met with heavy resistance. But when he realized that when God arises, His enemies are scattered, he strategically used this approach for ministry (see Ps. 68).

He split his team into two. One half went out to worship, and the other half would minister to people. The police told him that when he is on the streets, crime stops. This is an amazing result from a dove being released over a part of the city. The atmosphere changes as the presence is given His rightful place.

UNITED IN PRAISE

God loves the Church. He loves the idea, the potential, and everything to do with the Church, His Son's body on earth. In fact, He stated that zeal for this house has consumed Him! He has devoted His strength, wisdom, and His intense emotions to this house on earth—His eternal dwelling place.

What I've experienced with God at home on my own is priceless. I wouldn't trade it for anything in the world. But neither would I trade the amazing moments I've experienced through the years in the gatherings of hundreds or thousands. They are also priceless moments that prepare us for eternity when people from every tribe and tongue will lift up praises to the Lord. This is indescribable joy.

Some things are reserved for the individual. And yet some things are actually too precious to be given to only one. They must be shared with a company of people, a body—the Church. And there are aspects of His presence that will only be experienced in the corporate gathering. The exponential release and discovery of presence is equal to the size of the group of people united in the purpose of exalting Jesus in praise.

There are times when God will only allow us to recognize His presence in a crowd. It's not a rejection. He just longs for us to share His joy in the whole.

IN ALL BOLDNESS

When David became king, he sensed that God was looking for something else—priests who offer the sacrifices of thanksgiving and praise through the yielded and broken heart. This was done even though the Law he lived under forbade it. It was offered with musical instruments as well as the voices of the singers.

In this context, every priest could come daily before God without having to bring a blood offering. This order of worship was done twenty-four hours a day, seven days a week. This, of course, spoke of the day when every believer, a priest according to First Peter 2:9, would come to God in boldness because of what Jesus accomplished on our behalf. This is what was referred to when James said David's booth was being rebuilt.

PEOPLE OF HIS PRESENCE

King David would later discover some things about God's response to worship that were unknown in Moses' time. Each generation has access to more than the previous. It is God's law of compound interest. Specifically, David recognized how God responds to the praises of His people. God responds with His presence—He comes.

This call of God upon the nation of Israel was to leave Egypt in order to worship. They were becoming a people who would be known by the presence of God. He would become the distinguishing factor.

God's heart was for His entire nation of Israel to become priests. In fact, He commanded Moses to tell

Israel of His desire. *"And you shall be to Me a kingdom of priests and a holy nation"* (Exod. 19:6). Priests minister to God. The plan of God having a people of His presence was well underway.

A WORSHIPING COMMUNITY

E very time I read in Scripture that there are people ministering to Him and then there's a response from Heaven, I get excited. The lessons are always profound, as there's something of eternity on those moments. It doesn't matter whether it happened with David, Moses, or someone in the New Testament; those interactions are eternal in nature. And so it is with this next story.

> *It came even to pass, as the trumpeters and singers were as one, to make one sound to be heard in praising and thanking the Lord; and **when they lifted up their voice** with the trumpets and cymbals and instruments of*

musick, **and praised the Lord, saying, For he is good;** *for his mercy endureth for ever: that* **then the house was filled with a cloud,** *even the house of the Lord; so that the priests could not stand to minister by reason of the cloud: for* **the glory of the Lord had filled the house of God.**

(2 Chronicles 5:13-14 KJV)

Please note that the priests were offering the fruit of the lips (see Heb. 13:15) as their offering. While this happened in the Old Testament, it is clearly a New Testament practice, as the Law required the sacrifice of animals from the priests, not praise.

Second, notice that the priests were in unity. Remember that the 120 believers in Acts chapters 1 and 2 were also in unity before the outpouring of the Holy Spirit took place. God once again put His glory upon a united people (see Ps. 13). God loves to manifest Himself upon His people when we're known for our love of each other.

Third, look at what they were praising God for—His goodness! Becoming a worshiping community that worships in spirit, in truth, and in unity will offer something to Him that He in turn will want to occupy—the praises of His people concerning His goodness.

A PASSIONATE
HEART OF PRAISE

King David towers above all other Old Testament figures in this sense—he is remembered not so much for the greatness of his actions, but for the greatness of his heart for God. His passionate heart set him apart in God's eyes long before he ever won great military victories, before he revolutionized the nature of worship in Israel, or even ushered in Israel's Golden Age of economic and spiritual prosperity. While David was still in obscurity, God saw that he was a man after His own heart (see Acts 13:22).

What was the evidence of David's heart after God? Scripture indicates two primary aspects of David's life before he was anointed king. First, when nobody was looking, when nobody was calling prayer meetings or leading a revival in Judah, David was pouring out his heart in worship and prayer to God in the fields where he tended his father's sheep. With no one around, his pursuit of God was motivated by nothing but a desire to know God for His own sake.

David's relationship with the Lord was highly unusual for his day because the entire paradigm for worship in Israel at the time was focused on the sacrifice of animals to temporarily deal with sin, not the sacrifice of praise from the heart. His heart led him beyond the letter of the law to the heart of the Lord Himself. Second, David's battles against the lion and the bear revealed his heart for God because he relied completely on God for victory. This trust indicated that David's heart for the Lord was not something that changed according to his circumstances. He had integrity of heart (see 1 Sam. 17:37).

WORSHIP

Since we are receiving our rights to an unshakeable kingdom we should be extremely thankful and offer God the purest worship that delights his heart as we lay down our lives in absolute surrender, filled with awe. For our God is a holy, devouring fire!

—Hebrews 12:28-29 TPT

But an hour is coming, and now is, when the true worshipers will worship the Father in spirit and truth; for such people the Father seeks to be His worshipers. God is spirit, and those who worship Him must worship in spirit and truth.

—John 4:23-24 NASB

Therefore I urge you, brothers and sisters, by the mercies of God, to present your bodies [dedicating all of yourselves, set apart] as a living sacrifice, holy and well-pleasing to God, which is your rational (logical, intelligent) act of worship. And do not be conformed to this world [any longer with its superficial values and customs], but be transformed and progressively changed [as you mature spiritually] by the renewing of your mind [focusing on godly values and ethical attitudes], so that you may prove [for yourselves] what the will of God is, that which is good and acceptable and perfect [in His plan and purpose for you].

—Romans 12:1-2 AMP

Does the Lord delight in burnt offerings and sacrifices as much as in obeying the Lord? To obey is better than sacrifice, and to heed is better than the fat of rams.

—1 Samuel 15:22 NIV

EYES
TO SEE

God is very committed to teaching us how to see. To make this possible, He gave us the Holy spirit as a tutor. The curriculum that He uses is quite varied. But the one class we all qualify for is the greatest of all Christian privileges—worship. Learning how to see is not the purpose for our worship, but it is a wonderful byproduct.

Those who worship in spirit and truth, as mentioned in John 4:23-24, learn to follow the Holy Spirit's lead. His realm is called the Kingdom of God. The throne of God, which becomes established upon the praises of His people (see Ps. 22:3), is the center of that Kingdom. It's in the environment of worship that we learn things that go way beyond what our intellect can grasp (see Eph. 3:20)—and the greatest of these lessons is the value of His presence.

David was so affected by this that all his other exploits pale in comparison to his abandoned heart for God. We know that he learned to see into God's realm because of statements like, *"I have set the Lord always before me; because He is at my right hand I shall not be moved"* (Ps. 16:8). The presence of God affected his seeing. He would constantly practice recognizing the presence of God. He saw God daily, not with the natural eyes but with the eyes of faith. That priceless revelation was given to a worshiper.

The privilege of worship is a good beginning place for those unaccustomed to addressing some of these kinds of themes found in Scripture. It's in that wonderful ministry that we can learn to pay attention to this God-given gift—the ability to see with the heart. As we learn to worship with purity of heart, our eyes will continue to open. And we can expect to see what He wants us to see.

KINGDOM THINKING

You and I can be the most Kingdom-minded people on the planet when things are going well. We can see dozens healed, dozens saved, have great times of worship. But then I might go home and the car breaks down and suddenly I'm out $3,000.

Then the computer shuts off and the phone system goes out, and the neighbor's mad at me. The fire of circumstance expands whatever leaven is influencing my mind. Malachi 3:2 says, "*For He is like a refiner's fire.*" Malachi 4:1 says, "*For behold, the day is coming, burning like an oven.*" He is talking about a series of events that will draw certain influences to the surface where we can plainly see them—whether we like them or not.

I wish my first response to adversity was always to worship God with great faith. Sometimes it takes me a day or two, sometimes only a few minutes to get my heart and mind right. There are times when I get so troubled, so provoked and anxious, and I know biblically there is no reason for it. I always wonder, how can I be so worried and bogged down by pressures when He bought me with a price, gave me His Son, and will freely give me all things?

Kingdom thinking knows that anything is possible at any time. It's activated when you and I with tender hearts surrender to the thought patterns of God, when we receive His imaginations and say "yes." We want our minds to be full of Kingdom leaven, Kingdom influence. We want miracles, and we want those miracles to have their full effect on us, changing the way we see and behave.

OUR CENTRAL
RESPONSE

The apostle John once laid his head on the chest of Jesus. He was called the one whom Jesus loved. Toward the end of his life, on the isle of Patmos, he saw Jesus again. This time Jesus looked nothing like the one he shared that final meal with. His hair was white like wool, His eyes were a flame of fire, and His feet were like burnished bronze. God felt that this revelation was worthy of a book. It is called "The Revelation of Jesus Christ."

The entire Church will receive a fresh revelation of Jesus Christ, especially through that book. This that has been so mysterious will be understood. And that revelation will launch the Church into a transformation unlike any experienced in a previous age. Why? *Because as we see Him, we become like Him!*

If the revelation of Jesus is the primary focus of the Book of Revelation, then we'd also have to admit that worship is the central response. The coming increase in revelation of Jesus will be measurable through new dimensions of worship—corporate throne room experiences.

MINISTERING TO GOD

orship has become a primary part of life for me. I remember around 40 years ago, my dad did a teaching series on the subject of worship out of the Book of Ezekiel. He focused on what it was like to minister to God in the inner court and minister to people in the outer court.

I remember him teaching on this for several weeks, and at the end of one of the messages, I bowed my head and I prayed. There wasn't an altar call; there wasn't an invitation. It was just a very moving word, and I bowed my head. I said, "God, I give You the rest of my life to teach me this one thing. I want to know what it is to minister to You."

That has become such a predominant part of my life. Everything is focused around this one thing—to give Him glory. It's not just singing songs. It's not just rejoicing. All those are wonderful tools for giving Him glory, but worship is the goal.

I can stand in silence, in awe. I can shout and I can dance, in awe. Whatever the manifestation, I am overwhelmed by the One who is so kind and so good. Being a worshiper changes everything. Scripture says that God inhabits the praises of His people (see Ps. 22:3 KJV), so if we're going to be a presence-based culture, we have to be a worshiping culture. We have to be people who place worship as the top priority.

DISCIPLINED
IN WORSHIP

We don't worship so that we can get things from Him; we worship because of His worth. We worship because we acknowledge who He is. One translation of Psalm 22:3 is that He is *"enthroned"* upon the praises of His people. Believers who come daily before the Lord with lifted hands and a voice of praise, ministering to Him deeply and profoundly, are interacting with the presence and the glory of God in such a way that they are discipled to recognize the Holy Spirit.

We are being discipled in worship. God is mentoring us. He's mentoring us to be able to recognize His presence when He comes. Knowing how to recognize Him is vital so that we don't operate out of principle instead of presence. God wants us to sense the moving of His Holy Spirit. Otherwise, we can do a lot of well-intended things for God, based on principles of Scripture and really—at times—miss what He's actually doing.

ERASING THE DIVIDING LINE

I grew up at a time when those who were pastors, missionaries, and evangelists were considered to be *in the ministry*. They had sacred assignments because of their obvious responsibility to preach the Gospel. It seemed to escape our notice that every believer living the Gospel in the everyday affairs of life wasn't considered as important as preaching. Nor was there the same value for those with occupations that were not overtly spiritual. The thought that every believer was in ministry regardless of their occupation was foreign to most.

I remember so clearly when my dad and pastor began to teach that every believer was a priest unto the Lord (see 1 Pet. 2:9). This concept had been bantered around for centuries, but it has never really taken root in the measure that God intended. We needed to hear it again, this time at a whole new level.

That every believer was a priest unto the Lord was such a profound insight that it changed our lives completely. It started with the concept of worship. We learned that it was our privilege to minister to God with thanksgiving and praise and offer ourselves to Him in worship. It took a while, but soon the Church was truly embracing our assignment to minister to God. But still the line remained in people's thinking as it pertained to employment. That's the line that said one job was secular and the other was spiritual. For example, if someone worked in a school as a teacher of children, it was admired but was not considered spiritual. The same was true of any other occupation outside of public ministry.

In reality, there is no secular job for a believer. In all honesty, I've met people whose approach to their job in business is more holy than some I've known in their approach to pastoring. It's not the task that makes it holy. It is holy entirely based on the One who called us to that task, giving us His commission. His call is always holy. My approach to the call determines my effectiveness. Once we say yes to the responsibility, it is sanctified by the One who gave us the assignment.

WORK
AND WORSHIP

Moses was the one God liked to be with. What kind of assignment did God give to him? We know he was to bring Israel out of Egypt, out of the place of slavery to freedom. But what really was the heart of the assignment? *"Let My people go, that they may serve Me."* This is repeated numerous times (see Exod. 7:16; 8:1,20; 9:1,13; 10:3). This word *serve* is also used for the word *worship*.

Israel has a wonderful picture of the combination of work and worship in their experience that is rare in the Church's understanding today. The specific focus of this call was for Moses to bring Israel out of Egypt's captivity into another place in order that they might worship

God with sacrifices. It is appropriate that the one who would one day become a *face-to-face* man would be the one with this assignment.

GOD-INSPIRED LABOR

Many believers don't actually know how to live life in a practical way. They understand church attendance, serving in a ministry, and other essentials of that nature, but they really don't know how practical God is. They choose to give attention to what seems to be spiritual, never learning that the natural often reveals the nature of the unseen world.

When God gave Israel rules to live by, He was often showing them how His creation works. And to get His creation to serve you well, enabling you to prosper, they needed to pay attention to the rules of the designer.

It still astounds me that God's idea of paradise, the Promised Land, was a place where His people would have to work. Work is a pleasure in His eyes, and it is an expression of worship. Once again, we discover the subject of co-laboring with God. As we work, He breathes on our labor and the natural becomes supernaturally productive in ways that bless us and glorify Him.

This, of course, was under God's favor, but it was still work. In doing so, they would create wealth. God's idea of living on blessed land was to work hard and make blessed wages. God made His people to be the head and not the tail, the lender and not the borrower, and gave them the power to make wealth. Those realities are as true today as they've ever been. But people often misapply or misunderstand Jesus' teaching on money. Tragically, this misapplication of truth has cost generations their place of influence.

EXPRESSIONS
OF WORSHIP

L iving conscious of His delight in the simple things in life is key to a godly self-esteem. In turn, we are able to live in the strength intended from eating this heavenly meal called *obedience*. This could be misunderstood as performance for favor. It's not. This is the act of worship that comes from the favor we already have received. Healthy self-perception is the fruit.

Obedience is key in our understanding and affirming our identity. Jesus said, *"No longer do I call you slaves, for the slave does not know what his master is doing; but I have called you friends, for all things that I have heard from My Father I have made known to you"* (John 15:15 NASB). Having an identity as a friend of God has tremendous impact on our spiritual self-esteem, as it should.

But what preceded this statement was what gave us access to that friendship. *"You are My friends if you do what I command you"* (John 15:14 NASB). Obedience makes becoming a friend of God even possible. It is also how we prove our love for Him. *"If you love Me, you will keep My commandments"* (John 14:15 NASB).

If we don't know that caring for the poor or praying for the sick and tormented can be a part of our worship expression, we fail to draw upon our identity as friends of God called to change the world. Also, if we don't understand that going on a vacation with our family or watching our children and grandchildren in their sporting or musical activities is a part of our worship expression, we live below what God intended for us. We miss out on perceiving the face of a Father who delights in us, which is the great reward of this change in perspective.

When we stand before the Lord, we will watch as He honors those who have led millions to Christ or have served in a foreign land bringing the good news to people who otherwise never would have heard the Gospel.

But we will also see Him give a high place of honor to the couple who spent the bulk of their adult life caring for a handicapped child, or to those who over and over visited their parents or grandparents with Alzheimer's, who never once remembered their previous visit.

Things look different from His perspective. Only He can clearly see the beauty of a cup of water given in His name. Only He sees the heart of worship from the simplest of activities. And He rewards accordingly.

UNTO
THE LORD

We stand in God's presence, sometimes by the hour, honoring God with our thanksgiving and praise, responding to Him deeply in worship. It is a privilege beyond measure that we are invited into God's throne room to minister to Him. It is in this hallowed place that we tell Him how much we love Him. That is correctly called worship.

But He is the one who broadens the subject by suggesting that any time we do an act of kindness to another person, He receives it as unto Himself. Realizing this helps me to see that God wants me to do all that I do *as unto the Lord* and *with all of my might*—He calls it worship.

I knew that worship was more than the songs we sing to Him on a Sunday morning service, but little did I know that visiting someone in prison was worship. Little did I know that caring for the simplest of needs of my family is something He values as worship. A few years ago, I was told that Jews considered work to be one of their expressions of worship. This idea added much clarity to my thinking.

SHARING HIS FRAGRANCE

Remember the woman with the alabaster vial of perfume who ministered to Jesus? Scripture tells us two things about this vial: it was worth a year's wages (probably this woman's only financial security), and it could only be used on one occasion—because it was in a container that had to be broken to be opened.

Not only did she pour the entire contents on Jesus, she did it in a very public display of affection, weeping over His feet and wiping them with her hair. This extreme act provoked extreme offense in all who were present, including His disciples. They were embarrassed by her emotion and disgusted by the waste of money. But Jesus had a different perspective and response.

He explained that she had anointed Him for His burial, crediting her with more insight into His true identity than anyone else. She had given Him exactly the kind of worship He deserved, thereby demonstrating faith. And not only that, when everyone left the house, Jesus wasn't the only one drenched in the beautiful fragrance—the aroma encircled the woman as well.

This is what happens when we worship. We don't come to worship saying, "I'm giving this to You so we can share it." Like the woman, we worship to say, "Everything is Yours, God." But we can't come from that place of communion with Him without having who He is rub off on us.

David said that He is our glory and the lifter of our heads (see Ps. 3:3). We can't be with Him without having our heads lifted to see Him. And you can't look at Him and then look back at your circumstances with the same perspective. Also, you can't experience the realm of His glory, which is His realm of supernatural provision, without receiving a measure of His grace and strength.

THE BOOK
OF REMEMBRANCE

I'd be interested to know what is written in heaven's book of remembrance, but I think the record of Scripture gives us a good idea. Take the example of Sarah, Abraham's wife. In Genesis 18, she:

> *Laughed within herself, saying, "After I have grown old, shall I have pleasure, my lord being old also?" And the Lord said to Abraham, "Why did Sarah laugh, saying, 'Shall I surely bear a child, since I am old?' Is anything too hard for the Lord? At the appointed time I will return to you, according to the time of life, and Sarah shall have a son." But Sarah denied it,*

saying, "I did not laugh," for she was afraid.
And He said, "No, but you did laugh!"
                                    (Genesis 18:12-15)

She didn't just give an embarrassed giggle. The Hebrew word for *laugh* tells us she was *mocking* what God had said. Not only that, she lied about it when God confronted her.

But Hebrews 11:11 says of this same woman, *"By faith Sarah herself also received strength to conceive seed, and she bore a child when she was past the age, because she judged Him faithful who had promised."*

Wow! The record sure sounds different from the reality! This tells us something precious—the book of remembrance doesn't have a record of our mistakes. Genesis 18 was recorded for human benefit, so you and I could identify with those who followed God in the past. But Hebrews 11 is how it's recorded in the book of remembrance.

Once the blood has been applied, there is no record of sin anymore. God brags all over heaven about Sarah, and He does the same about you and me. Maybe you had a bad week, but you stirred yourself to worship God anyway. That was recorded in the book of remembrance.

You may have yelled at the kids all the way to church, but when you apologized and sincerely worshiped God and sought His presence, the angels recorded, "So-and-so moved in great faith on this date. She rose above difficult circumstances and saw the purposes of God that were superior to everything in her life." What looked in the natural like an awful Sunday morning was recorded as a great act of faith!

REQUEST
DENIED!

One of the primary ways that many believers need to be renewed in their perspective is by getting rid of the idea that intentionally ignoring the problems around them, and even within them, in order to give God praise and thanks is irresponsible. Believers often fall into the trap of thinking they can find a solution by looking at a problem from every angle and letting it consume their world. But what happens is that the affections of their hearts get drawn away from the Lord, to the point that they care more about the problem than about giving Him what He deserves. They are letting other voices speak louder than His, and that is always irresponsible!

I am responsible to Him first, and for this reason I have decided to live in a healthy state of denial. When the devil puts a request for attention across my desk, I say, "REQUEST DENIED!" I am aware that there are situations constantly around me that, if I'm not careful, can bring me into discouragement. Most of the time I'm living about 15 minutes away from discouragement if I make a series of wrong choices. But I also know that I never again have to live with discouragement like I used to.

I have learned to ignore problems just enough so they don't become a threat to the affections of my heart. I know I'm not being irresponsible because God has promised me over and over that if I'm faithful to be who He has called me to be, especially as a worshiper, He is more than happy to bring the solutions. This does not mean we are not to give attention to problems—but we need to address them from God's perspective.

ACCESS
TO HEAVEN

When we worship, we have access to the heavenly realm. When we worship, we push ourselves out of the inferior realms where we can pick up all of the negative stuff, and we end up in the glory realm, surrounded by His presence. I heard a story many years ago about a Christian man who was very depressed. He was so desperate for God to help him. He was crying out to God one day and heard the Lord tell him, "For a whole year, I want you to worship me."

God went on to tell him that He didn't want him to ask for anything when he prayed. Just worship. After that year, he was released from the depression that he had lived in for so long. I'm sure he learned a very valuable lesson in that year.

Someone asked my husband what his prayer life looked like. He said, "If I have an hour to spend praying, I will usually worship for around 45 minutes and pray the rest." It's amazing how many things you can pray for in ten to fifteen minutes."

WARFARE WORSHIP

Two elements in warfare that I feel are our greatest tools of intercession are worship and joy. I believe that these two weapons bring more confusion to the devil's camp than anything else. Both of these weapons of war come out of our intimate relationship with our Father God.

The Greek word for *worship* is *proskuneo;* it means "to kiss." It is a feeling or attitude within us that keeps us close to God. It is not just about coming to church on Sunday and singing songs during the worship service. Even though that is an important thing that we do together, it is not the most important thing. Worship comes from within us and goes with us throughout our day. When we adore God, we are kissing Him. Warfare worship is coming in on God's terms, not the devil's. We are focused on God, which ushers His power and presence into our intercessions.

I was in one of our worship services one Sunday morning, and I kept getting distracted in my spirit. I felt like there were some witches in the room. I found myself completely out of worship. I remember, I kept turning around to look to see if I could figure out what was going on. I did this a few times. Then I heard Holy Spirit whisper, "You are being distracted from Me; just worship Me." It was a little nudge from the Spirit, but I got it.

I realized that what I needed to do was just be with God and worship. He would take care of the spiritual matters in the room. My weapon of warfare that morning was to worship Him. God once spoke audibly to my husband (Bill) saying, "He watches over the watch of those who watch the Lord." It is clear that having our eyes fixed on Him is our most responsible position, as God watches over the things that matter to us.

THE HOUSE
OF GOD

We, the Church, the redeemed, are the tabernacle of the Holy Spirit, the eternal dwelling place of God! We are living stones, according to First Peter 2:4-5, fitly framed together, building the eternal dwelling place of God. The House of God is us!

If we understand and are confident in our identity as the House of God, we can do great exploits. No power of darkness in any realm of creation can stop our fellowship with the Father. There is an open heaven over each one of us, from the newest Christian to the most mature.

Being the House of God means we have the exact authority Jesus has at the right hand of the Father. We are entitled and empowered to be His "House," His embodiment on earth. As a Christian at this very moment, you have absolute liberty and access to heaven.

I have been to many cities that are known for their darkness. Yet the practices of occult leaders cannot block the open heaven over any believer who abides in Christ. Even the demoniac, as tormented as he was, couldn't be stopped from his "God encounter" as he fell at Jesus' feet in worship!

I never notice the lack of an open heaven unless I become impressed with the devil's accomplishments in that city. To be the House of God, we must bustle and brim with the life, joy, healing, and peace that is normal in heaven. We must set our hearts on being a House filled with His glory wherever we go.

HEAVEN'S
AMBASSADORS

The Lord's Prayer provides the clearest instruction on how we bring the reality of His world into this one. The generals of revival speak to us from ages past, saying, *If you pray, He will come!* Biblical prayer is always accompanied by radical obedience. God's response to prayer with obedience always releases the nature of heaven into our impaired circumstances.

Jesus' model reveals the only two real priorities of prayer: first, intimacy with God that is expressed in worship—*holy is Your name.* And second, to bring His Kingdom to earth, establishing His dominion over the needs of mankind—*Your Kingdom come.*

As disciples, we are both citizens and ambassadors of another world. This world is our assignment, but not our home. Our purpose is eternal. The resources needed to complete the assignment are unlimited. The only restrictions are those between our ears.

THE NORMAL CHRISTIAN LIFE

In our school of ministry, we train people in signs and wonders and are especially keen to learn how to operate in the supernatural outside the four walls of the church. We encourage our students by giving them specific assignments to invite God to work in public places.

One day after class, a bunch of students from our worship school went to visit a lady in the hospital. She had a brain tumor, was deaf in one ear, and was losing feeling on the right side of her body. She spoke with great difficulty, slurring her words, and she was in terrible pain. Instead of laying hands on her and praying, the students surrounded her in worship, singing songs, expressing their love to the Lord.

Pretty soon the woman said, "My ears opened!" The deafness had left. They kept singing and she said, "My speech is clearer!" She started speaking clearly. Pretty soon she was moving her limbs around. She exclaimed, "All the pain is gone!" God overhauled her body when a worship service broke out around her.

When we do the will of God, we bring Kingdom reality crashing into the works of the devil. We initiate conflict between earthly reality and heavenly reality, becoming the bridge and connection point that makes it possible through prayer and radical obedience to assert the rulership of God.

Not long ago, a woman with a broken arm came to our church with her wrist in such pain that we couldn't even touch her skin to pray for it. We held our hands away and prayed, and within moments God healed it completely. She had no pain and was twisting the wrist all around. The arm was totally different than it had been seconds earlier. Kingdom reality had overwhelmed one of the devil's works. *That's* the normal Christian life.

TRUE
WORSHIPERS

When we worship, we can release the presence of God and His Kingdom into the room. Years ago, we were doing some meetings in Alaska. For several of the meetings, during the praise and worship time, there was no worship part. The praise was good, but we weren't getting to the intimate place of worship. It felt like there was a wall between us and God.

We had brought our lead dancer with us on this trip. She is fun to take on trips because of the worship that she expresses when she dances. When we want something broken in the spirit realm, we have her get up and just worship. She doesn't dance to war, but her dance of worship becomes war. We don't even tell her what is going on. We just want her to worship. After being in a couple of these services in Alaska, my husband thought that it would be a good time for her to dance. She got up and began dancing, and whatever the wall was, it disappeared, and Heaven came into the room.

Worship, in whatever form—dance, adoration that comes from our mouth, or any other kind of worship— terrifies the demonic realm. I believe they cannot stand to hear or even be close to those who are true worshipers. I've watched our son Brian take his guitar and play over a person in torment to see peace come. I know of a woman who goes to the convalescent hospital in our city and plays her flute over Alzheimer's patients to watch them become peaceful.

THE OVERFLOW
OF WORSHIP

Angels are impressive beings. They are glorious and powerful. So much so that when they showed up in Scripture, people often fell to worship them. While it is foolish to worship them, it is equally foolish to ignore them. Angels are assigned to serve wherever we serve, if the supernatural element is needed. *"Are not all angels ministering spirits sent to serve those who will inherit salvation?"* (Heb. 1:14 NIV).

When God chose to bring the Messiah through the virgin Mary, He sent Gabriel the angel to bring the message. When the apostle Paul was about to suffer shipwreck, an angel of the Lord told him what would happen. On numerous occasions throughout Scripture, angels did what God could have done easily Himself. But why didn't God do those things Himself?

For the same reason He doesn't preach the gospel— He has chosen to let His creation enjoy the privilege of service in His Kingdom. Service with purpose affirms identity. A godly self-esteem is derived from doing "as He pleases." And true service is an overflow of worship.

OUR FIRST
MINISTRY

Our first ministry is to God. He has made us a dwelling place for His Spirit. As we behold Him, we are moved to worship with joyous passion. God delights in us and He has always desired to be with us. We focus on His presence because we have discovered that He is focused on us. Being focused on His presence doesn't mean Christians should spend all their time in private worship, though.

Purposefully cultivating a hunger for God's manifest presence and an openness to experiencing the Holy Spirit deepens our friendship with God and our awareness that we carry His presence for the sake of the world. Every part of a Christian's life is sacred and meant to be holy.

We do not live with the false mindset that life is divided into the "sacred" or the "secular." Rather, God is involved in and valued in every area of our lives. The Holy Spirit lives in us, so everything we do and everywhere we go is sacred. As a lifestyle, we practice recognizing God's presence while we minister to others, attempting to say what He is saying and do what He is doing.

CAPTIVATED
BY THE ONE

We are to bring transformation to the world, but we do so because we are people of the presence. We're people of the glory. We've had times in our gatherings when the glory of God comes so strongly that I refuse to go up and teach. I believe in the teaching of the Word. We do it day after day. It's a huge part of our value system.

But there are times when we've been worshiping for an extended period of time and His glory begins to fill the room in such a way that there is no way I'm going to go up and teach. I'm not going to interrupt God with my ideas. And, of course, there are other times that the glory of God is so strong that that's exactly what needs to be done. Other times we simply stand there or kneel for 20 minutes—no song, nothing being done.

The point is, we are in awe. We are captivated by the One, the only One who has the right to rule over our lives.

A CONTRITE AND THANKFUL HEART

Even before Christ came, there was someone who followed in Moses' footsteps and chose to "[draw] *near the thick darkness where God was*" (Exod. 20:21). David was a unique individual in the Old Testament because he discovered the hidden dimensions of God's higher will for His relationship with His people. He discovered that God didn't really want the blood of bulls and goats but the sacrifice of a contrite and thankful heart.

This discovery led him to do something unimaginable. He took the Ark of the Covenant, the Ark that only the High Priest was allowed to see once a year, and brought it into a tabernacle of his own design, where he had priests worshiping around it 24 hours a day for years.

He didn't do this casually, especially after a man died in the initial attempt to bring the Ark to Jerusalem on a cart. But his heart for the presence of God led him to establish a personal, passionate expression of worship before the Ark that, technically, should have been illegal for a man who was not a priest, or even for anyone who lived before the blood of Jesus was shed.

FOCUSED ON HIS WORTHINESS

We are often more convinced of our *unworthiness* than we are of His *worth*. Our *inability* takes on greater focus than does His *ability*. But the same One who called *fearful Gideon* a "valiant warrior" and *unstable Peter* a "rock" has called us the Body of His beloved Son on earth. That has to count for something. The very fact that He declares it makes the impossible possible.

Those who walk in arrogance because of how they see themselves in Christ don't really see it at all. When we see who He is, what He has done on our behalf, and who He says we are, there is only one possible response—worship from a humble and surrendered heart.

ALIGNMENT—SPIRIT, SOUL, AND BODY

I know that worshiping aligns my spirit and soul with God. I also believe that it aligns my body with Heaven, because we are triune beings—body, mind, and spirit are all one. I have experienced firsthand how being in the presence of God has really enabled my body to heal.

This makes me think of a friend who came to speak at a service being held at our church. Although very few people knew at the time, she was struggling with serious health issues. While she was speaking, it seemed that every few minutes she would pause briefly. I asked her after the service what she was doing and she showed me that she had what she called an "invisible clock."

A doctor in Europe had recommended it for his cancer patients. He would have them set it to vibrate every ten minutes, and every time it vibrated they would worship God. I thought this was a genius idea. We tend to get so caught up in the hustle and bustle of our lives that it's easy to forget to talk to God. This invisible clock reminds us to posture our heart in reverence to Him.

I immediately purchased one, and began wearing it every day—and worshiping. After about three weeks, I woke up one morning, and the first thing I noticed was how good I felt. I realized that even though I hadn't been aware of it, I had been feeling slightly depressed. I don't mean the chronic depression that many people deal with, but the less serious kind that comes from being overworked and overtired. My daily, conscious effort to worship had brought my spirit and soul into alignment, and my body quickly followed.

DECLARED BY WORSHIPERS

Psalms is the great book of worship. Songs were written to exalt God. But something unique happened in a few of these psalms. The writer would start to make declarations about the nations rising up to give God glory. Decrees were made about every nation worshiping the one true God. Read these verses below:

All the ends of the earth will remember and turn to the Lord, and all the families of the nations will worship before You.

(Psalm 22:27 NASB)

Let the nations be glad and sing for joy; for You will judge the peoples with uprightness and guide the nations on the earth.

(Psalm 67:4 NASB)

May His name endure forever; may His name increase as long as the sun shines; and let men bless themselves by Him; let all nations call Him blessed.

(Psalm 72:17 NASB)

All nations whom You have made shall come and worship before You, O Lord, and they shall glorify Your name.

(Psalm 86:9 NASB)

Praise the Lord, all nations; laud Him, all peoples!

(Psalm 117:1 NASB)

Worshipers are the ones who first declare God's plans for the nations. Why? Worshipers are in a place to call nations into their purpose, into their God-given destiny. It is the sacred privilege of those who worship.

SETTING
HIS FACE

Second Chronicles 20 gives us insight into a strategy where worship was used to win a battle. Jehoshaphat was faced with a great army coming against all of Judah. The first thing that Jehoshaphat did was to seek the Lord and proclaim a fast: "*And Jehoshaphat feared, and set himself to seek the Lord, and proclaimed a fast throughout all Judah*" (2 Chron. 20:3).

I like this verse because it says he "set himself" to seek the Lord. That means he set his face. I can see Jehoshaphat turning with an attitude of *I will not turn away until I have heard from God*. I like the courage and determination in this king's heart. The second thing that happened was that they prayed. The people came from everywhere to fast and ask the Lord what they should do. The Bible says, "*So Judah gathered together to ask help from the Lord; and from all the cities of Judah they came to seek the Lord*" (2 Chron. 20:4).

They began their prayer with adoring God for who He was and is: "*O Lord God of our fathers, are You not God in heaven, and do You not rule over all the kingdoms of the nations, and in Your hand is there not power and might, so that no one is able to withstand You?*" (2 Chron. 20:6). They were saying to God, "You are great and there is no one else."

SETTING
HIS FACE (2)

Are You not our God, who drove out the inhabitants of this land before Your people Israel, and gave it to the descendants of Abraham Your friend forever? And they dwell in it, and have built You a sanctuary in it for Your name, saying, "If disaster comes upon us—sword, judgment, pestilence, or famine— we will stand before this temple and in Your presence (for Your name is in this temple), and cry out to You in our affliction, and You will hear and save."

(2 Chronicles 20:7-9)

It feels like they are reminding God of who He is and what He has done for His people. It also looks like they are reminding themselves of who God is and what He has done. That is a good habit to have—always bringing the testimony of God before us to remind us of His greatness.

In verse 9, Jehoshaphat talks about going into the temple and into God's presence (see 2 Chron. 20:9). The prayer gets pretty desperate in verse 12: "*O our God, will You not judge them? For we have no power against this great multitude that is coming against us; nor do we know what to do, but our eyes are upon You*" (2 Chron. 20:12).

They basically said, "They are coming against us, and we just don't know what to do, but our eyes are on You." Ever pray that prayer? You just don't know what to do or how to even pray? At times like this, such brokenness goes on in us. This brokenness must lead us to God, not away from Him. We must set our eyes upon the One who is true and trust Him.

SETTING HIS FACE (3)

The third thing that happened in the story of Jehoshaphat was that they worshiped the Lord. God had answered His people, and in return they bowed before the Lord and worshiped. There was a praise that rose up in the congregation. And the fourth thing that happened was that they praised the Lord.

That word *praise* is translated from the Hebrew word *tehillah,* which comes from the Hebrew root word *hallel. Tehillah* is "to praise" and *hallel* is "to be boastful, act insanely, drive madly, *giving praises.*" This was their time to let loose, to give wild praise to their God.

Jehoshaphat told the people to believe in the Lord and to believe in the prophets. He appointed those who should sing to the Lord and who should praise the beauty of holiness.

And when he had consulted with the people, he appointed those who should sing to the Lord, and who should praise the beauty of holiness, as they went out before the army and were saying: "Praise the Lord, for His mercy endures forever." Now when they began to sing and to praise, the Lord set ambushes against the people of Ammon, Moab, and Mount Seir, who had come against Judah; and they were defeated. For the people of Ammon and Moab stood up against the inhabitants of Mount Seir to utterly kill and destroy them. And when they had made an end of the inhabitants of Seir, they helped to destroy one another. So when Judah came to a place overlooking the wilderness, they looked toward the multitude; and there were their dead bodies, fallen on the earth. No one had escaped. When Jehoshaphat and his people came to take away their spoil, they found among them an abundance of valuables on the dead bodies, and precious jewelry, which they stripped off for themselves, more than they could carry away; and they were three days gathering the spoil because there was so much.

(2 Chronicles 20:21-25)

The result—God set ambushes so that, by the time the people of God got to the battle, the war was over. This is such an amazing story of a strategy of trusting God and letting praise and worship go before and win the fight. The Bible says, "*They returned, every man of Judah and Jerusalem, with Jehoshaphat in front of them, to go back to Jerusalem with joy, for the Lord had made them rejoice over their enemies*" (2 Chron. 20:27). The people of God fought a war by worship. Their worship set in motion a shift in the heavenly realm, and God did the rest.

FULFILLING
OUR MANDATE

The Bible frequently speaks of the responsibilities given to those who follow Jesus. But there is one assignment given that is so large, encompassing, that every other commission aligns its purpose to the fulfillment of that one. Perhaps we could call the other assignments *sub-points to one major point*. Each commission is vital and important because it serves the greater purpose. And the fulfillment is the realization of God's dream through the cooperation of those made in His image.

Our assignment as believers is a mandated focus that is to influence our relational journey with God. This becomes most evident in the discovery that our commission is to pray. And that prayer has a specific focus that is to become a vital part of our fellowship with God. Simply put, in the context of drawing near to our Father in worship and interaction, we are to lift up our voices, declaring, *"Your kingdom come, your will be done, on earth as it is in heaven"* (Matt. 6:10 NIV).

THE BACKSIDE
OF THE DESERT

King David is known for many wonderful things throughout Scripture. He was a great king who led Israel into their greatest hour. He was a man after God's heart. He proved this long before he became king. Even his bravery was proven long before he was seated upon the throne.

His courage against the lion and the bear when no one was watching set him up for the victory over Goliath when two entire nations were watching. This set the pace for his profound leadership with the people of God—one of extraordinary courage.

But the one thing that was the primary reference point in all of his life was his passion for the presence of God. I think that his biggest mark on history was the standard he set as a worshiper. It was his worship that sculpted the heart of a nation into a nation who valued the presence of God. As Moses once declared, it was the presence of God upon His people that became the distinguishing mark that separated them from all other nations (see Exod. 33:16).

David was a worshiper on the backside of the desert caring for his father's sheep. This wasn't done for performance or status. It was the purest expression of his heart and became the reason for God choosing him above his brothers as the ruler over Israel.

PERSONAL
WORSHIP

My prayer times are less and less about issues of need, and more and more about discovering this wonderful Person who has given Himself so freely and completely to me. Worship has become a primary part of life. It's wonderful when it's in the corporate gathering. But it's shallow when it's only corporate.

My personal life must be one of continuous worship to experience the transformations that I long for. We always become like the one we worship.

I still believe in prayer and intercession. It is a joy. But my heart has this bent toward the presence that is bigger than the answers I am seeking. There's a Person to be discovered, daily. He must be enjoyed, and discovered yet again. And it's all His idea. I can seek Him only because He found me.

GIVING US
THE OPTION

God didn't create us to be robots. He made us to be powerful expressions of Himself. When He did this, He made it possible for Him to feel heartache and pain from our choices. All parents understand this pain. He took a risk by giving us a choice to serve Him, ignore Him, or even mock Him.

The Perfect One chose vulnerability, a willingness to be influenced by what He has made, over the squeaky-clean world that the robots could manage without disrupting His plan. Why did He consider it worth the risk? What was He looking for? People, those made in His image, who took their place before Him as worshipers, as sons and daughters, as those whose very natures are immersed in His. They would become co-laborers in managing, creating, and contributing to the well-being of all He has made. From His perspective it was worth the risk.

Our freedom of choice is so valuable to Him that He restrains Himself from manifesting His presence in a way where our freedom of choice would be removed. That may sound strange to some, but when He reveals Himself in fullness, even the devil and his demons will declare that Jesus Christ is Lord. Some realities are so overwhelming, like the full manifestation of God's glory, that there's little room for reason and choice.

God has chosen to veil Himself in just the right measure so that our wills and intellects could be shaped by our allegiance to Him. He is there for anyone humble enough to recognize his or her personal need. He is also subtle enough to be ignored by those who are filled with themselves.

PLEASING
GOD'S HEART

There is no question that spending time with God changes our desires. We always become like the one we worship. But it's not because we've been programmed to wish for the things He wants us to wish for; it's because in friendship we discover the things that please Him—the secret things of His heart.

It is the instinct of the true believer to search for and find that which brings pleasure to the Father. Our nature actually changes at conversion. It is our new nature to seek to know God and to please Him with our thoughts, ambitions, and desires.

ADDRESSING PRIORITIES

I was given an unusual mandate that I had never heard anyone teach on or explain: *When God is number one, there is no number two.* This would end up changing most every area of my life, as it reveals God's approach to our lives in ways that the wonderful list of priorities never could.

I honestly felt that I heard the Lord speak that phrase to me—*When God is number one, there is no number two.* It started to make sense to me that as long as I had a list of priorities, I'd have to leave my first priority to do the second, and so on. This new insight implied I could only serve God. I guess that's logical. But the implications were life-changing, as I had to learn how those things could become a part of my service to God. All of those things were to be an offering to Him.

Every area of my life must be part of my worship of God Himself. If there's a part of my life that cannot be an expression of my love for God, it shouldn't be in my life.

This change in perspective didn't change my practice as much as it changed my confidence that I was delighting God's heart. I always made family first. But what I didn't realize was how much God was being loved through my love for my wife and children. There is no vacation from God. I don't stop my service to God while I serve people. It's actually quite the opposite. He takes it personally. Something happens when you realize that what you're doing brings pleasure to His heart. Our personal esteem and confidence grow dramatically.

A LIVING
SACRIFICE

Holiness is more powerful than sin; it's the purity of Christ in you. The apostle Paul demonstrates this process in Romans, which is considered the greatest theological treatise on the subject of our salvation. The first eleven chapters deal with theology and doctrine, while chapters 12 through 16 deal mostly with our conduct. A quick overview of some of the highlights in chapter 12 gives us an interesting perspective on true Kingdom attitudes that bring about change in society.

In Paul's very first statement, he declares that we are to be living offerings of worship (see Rom. 12:1). Worship is to be a primary focus that affects all we are and do.

That is the context for the development of the renewed mind (see Rom. 12:2), which is absolutely essential to manifest God's Kingdom. Giving ourselves to God in worship as a living sacrifice is the context of getting our minds renewed.

BECOMING LIKE HIM

Worship is powerful for many reasons. One of the most important is that we always become like the One we worship. This by itself would take Israel to new levels. But this call of God upon the nation of God would not go unnoticed.

The devil is very afraid of a worshiping people. He actually doesn't mind complacent worship, as it seems to work opposite to the real thing—it deadens our sensitivities to the Holy Spirit of God. It works completely opposite to the effects of sold out, passionate worship. Complacent worship is an oxymoron.

CONVENIENCE
VS. SACRIFICE

Satan's strategy against God's people and their call as God's intimates has never been clearer than when he revealed his hand through Pharaoh's words: *"Go, sacrifice to your God within the land"* (Exod. 8:25 NASB).

Convenience and sacrifice cannot coexist. The *going* is a sacrifice, and a non-sacrificial people are of no consequence to the devil. The enemy knows there's power in the offering and will do whatever he can to distract us from giving it. Sometimes we fail to reach our destiny because we insist on it happening where we are—within reason, with little effort involved on our end. We often cannot get to a new place in worship until we get to a new place in God.

I've heard so many people say through the years, "If it is God's will to move powerfully in my life (or church), He knows we're hungry, and He knows where we are." Foolishness! He's not a cosmic bellhop, bouncing around the universe to fulfill our every wish. He has a plan. And we must move into His plan. Wise men still travel, both in the natural and figuratively speaking.

DISREGARD FOR THE PRESENCE

Michal, the daughter of Saul, looked out through the palace window at David dancing before the presence of God as it entered Jerusalem. Extreme worship always looks to be extreme foolishness to those who stand at a distance. Some things can only be understood from within. Such is the case with authentic worship.

Michal was appalled at David's lack of regard for how people perceived his passion, his humility in attire, and his complete lack of public decorum. Instead of greeting him with honor, she tried to shame him.

His response was very bold in many ways:

> *So David said to Michal, "It was before the*
> *Lord, who chose me above your father and*
> *above all his house, to appoint me ruler over the*
> *people of the Lord, over Israel; therefore I will*
> *celebrate before the Lord. I will be more lightly*
> *esteemed than this and will be humble in my*
> *own eyes, but with the maids of whom you have*
> *spoken, with them I will be distinguished."*
>
> (2 Samuel 6:21-22 NASB)

David made it clear that God chose him above her father. This was a biting comment to say the least. Her disregard for the presence of God revealed that she carried some of the same *lack of value* for the presence that her father Saul had lived by during his reign. Dumbing down our emphasis on the presence should never be to accommodate the Michals in the house. He followed that comment stating that she basically hadn't seen anything yet. In other words, if that embarrassed her, her future was not too bright. David was just getting warmed up.

BARRENNESS/
FRUITFULNESS

Whenever someone despises extravagant worship, they put themselves in an extremely dangerous position. Michal had scorned David's extravagant worship. Tragically, *"Michal the daughter of Saul had no child to the day of her death"* (2 Sam. 6:23 NASB).

Barrenness is the natural result of despising worship. In doing so they are rejecting the reason why we're alive. Barrenness and the absence of worship go hand in hand. This scene happened again during Jesus' ministry. It was when the costly ointment was poured over Jesus. All the disciples were upset (see Matt. 26:8). The devil actually doesn't mind worship that is tame. Extreme worship exposes religion in everyone.

There is a wonderful verse that speaks to the effect of extreme worship on barrenness itself.

> *"Shout for joy, O barren one, you who have borne no child; break forth into joyful shouting and cry aloud, you who have not travailed; for the sons of the desolate one will be more numerous than the sons of the married woman,"* says the Lord.
>
> (Isaiah 54:1 NASB)

What a promise. In this chapter we find a barren woman who is exhorted to shout for joy *before* she becomes pregnant. The end result is that she will have more children than the one who has been having children all along. This provides quite the prophetic picture. The people who are people of worship, regardless of circumstances, will become fruitful in ways beyond reason.

Anyone can get happy after the miracle has come. Show me someone who celebrates before the answer, and I'll show you someone who is about to experience the answer. This is the nature of faith—it looks ahead and lives accordingly.

Perhaps it would be appropriate to reintroduce the Genesis 1:28 passage in this context, as worshipers truly will *"be fruitful and multiply, and fill the earth, and subdue it"* (NASB). Is this example of Michal and the Isaiah 54 woman really that significant? I believe it is.

In David's Tabernacle, we are connected to our original purpose as worshipers to be carriers of the glory and restore fruitfulness to the barren places in the lives of those who have suffered at the enemy's hands. The devil came to *"steal and kill and destroy"* (John 10:10 NASB). Jesus came to defeat the devil, expose his works, and reverse their effects. He came to give life. We have inherited that privileged assignment of enforcing the victory of Christ in those same ways. Worshipers just do that by nature.

IN HIS
LIKENESS

Everything God created was made for His pleasure. He is a God of extravagant joy. He enjoys everything He made. Humanity has a unique place in His creation, though, in that we are the only part of His creation actually made like God. Likeness was made for the purpose of fellowship—intimate communion.

Through relationship with God, the finite ones would be grafted into His eternal perfect past and obtain through promise an eternal perfect future. Even the realm of impossibilities could be breached by those created to be like Him. *"All things are possible to him who believes"* (Mark 9:23). No other part of creation has been given access to that realm. We have been invited in a "place" known only by God.

The heart of God must be celebrated at this point—He longs for partnership. He risked everything to have that one treasure—those who would worship Him, not as robots, not merely out of command, but out of relationship.

ALL
ABOUT HIM

The offering from convenience protects form, ritual, and image. None of these things threaten the devil. He'll even attend the meetings where such priorities exist. And strangely, he'll go unnoticed. True worship involves my whole being. It is physical, emotional, spiritual, intellectual, and financial. It involves my relationships and my family, and it has a major impact on the boundaries I've set for how I want to live.

Worship has a complete focus—God and His worth. It really is all about Him. It's about presence. Israel, a generation of slaves at this point, was called to greatness. And their first step into such greatness was to worship

Him extravagantly! *"Go, serve the Lord as you have said"* (Exod. 12:31). Every plague, every act of violence and opposition to the enemies of God, is simply God sparing no expense to preserve what is important to Him—an intimate people who worship.

Mike Bickle says it best—*all of God's judgments are aimed at that which interferes with love.* But this part of the story doesn't end here. We've seen that people are called to put everything on the line as they seek to follow God as worshipers. Just a few verses later we see how God rewarded them. *"And the Lord had given the people favor...thus they plundered the Egyptians"* (Exod. 12:36). Just when you think you gave up everything to follow God, He gives you more to offer.

THE EXAMPLE OF DAVID

No one in Scripture embraced the *culture-shaping value* of the testimony as did David. Testimonies were his counselors, his meditation at night, his pursuit in study, and his inheritance. Testimonies were so important that he made sure that Solomon, the son who would be king, was groomed on this diet.

> But chose the tribe of Judah, Mount Zion which He loved. And He built His sanctuary like the heights, like the earth which He has established forever. He also chose David His servant, and took him from the sheepfolds; from following the ewes that had young He brought him, to shepherd Jacob His people, and Israel His

inheritance. So he shepherded them according to the integrity of his heart, and guided them by the skillfulness of his hands.

(Psalm 78:68-72)

It is also no mistake that the one known for a life of worship was so extremely devoted to living under the influence of the works of God. When you see the wonder of God through His works, you can't help but become the living offering in worship.

Israel had occasional success and much failure. Their success seemed to depend on the integrity of those in charge. While there were other righteous leaders in Israel's history besides David, none made the impact, according to the principles of grace found in the New Testament, that he did.

The introduction of David in this psalm reminds us that more than any leader in history, he represents a heavenly culture—the kind that great kingdoms are known for. His example was the answer for the continual failings of a people who throughout this psalm had lost their sense of purpose and direction, both of which had been reinforced by their history of God's supernatural interventions.

David's abandonment in worship represented his affinity to the realities of Heaven permeating his life. That is the nature of the life of one who lives to release the power of that world into this one.

LEARNING ON THE JOURNEY

Saul was the king before David. As King Saul had little regard for the presence of God (Ark of the Covenant), David became king of Judah and then Israel. He was acquainted with the presence of God from his time on the backside of the desert, caring for his father's sheep.

He was a worshiper. He no doubt learned of God's desire for yielded hearts instead of the blood of bulls and goats in his private times with God. Some of God's best lessons can't be learned in a class; they can only be learned on a journey.

IN LINE WITH
SOLOMON

The relationship between David and Solomon—the generational transfer of wisdom and purpose—is a prophetic picture of Christ and the Church. David began to establish in the kingdom of Israel a foundation that involved an entirely different approach to His presence.

Solomon built upon his father's foundation and brought that kingdom to a mature expression of worship and social life. Similarly, Christ, the Son of David, ushered in the Kingdom of God, and has entrusted the Church with the commission to co-labor and co-create with the Holy Spirit to establish that Kingdom on earth as it is in Heaven.

This is the responsibility of every believer. God has given us a role that put us directly in line with Solomon when it comes to the priority of pursuing divine wisdom. He has called us to be kings and priests (see Rev. 1:5). This role is to *re-present* the King and His Kingdom and, in so doing, to bring earthly reality into alignment with Heaven.

REBUILDING THE
TABERNACLE

There's a prophecy declared both by Isaiah and Micah that has spoken to my heart now for many years. It speaks of the mountain of God's house. This can be none other than Mount Zion. This is prophetically fulfilled in the last days. I believe that it is referring to the rebuilding of the Tabernacle of David—the New Testament combining of believers from all nations into one company of people called worshipers.

> *Now it will come about that in the last days*
> *the mountain of the house of the Lord will*
> *be established as the chief of the mountains,*

*and will be raised above the hills; and all the
nations will stream to it.*

(Isaiah 2:2 NASB; see also Micah 4:1)

Look at the effect of this house being established as
chief of all mountains. *Chief* means *head*. This government will be the head of all governments. As a result, all
nations will stream to it, asking for the word of the Lord.
I believe this is referring to the massive harvest that will
take place before the end comes. It is brought about
by worshipers. It is the rebuilding of the Tabernacle of
David. Worship affects the destiny of nations.

PROPHETIC PROTOTYPE

"In that day I will raise up the fallen booth of David, and wall up its breaches; I will also raise up its ruins and rebuild it as in the days of old; that they may possess the remnant of Edom and all the nations who are called by My name," declares the Lord who does this.

(Amos 9:11-12 NASB)

Notice that the rebuilding of this tabernacle, known for the abiding presence of God and the worship from the priests, coincides with Gentiles being added to the faith. There is a connection in the unseen realm between the effect of worship and the conversion of souls.

The Tabernacle of David changed the focus of life and ministry for all priests in the Old Testament. It's a good thing, too. In the New Testament, we discover that every believer is now a priest unto the Lord (see 1 Pet. 2:9). The Old Testament priesthood would be impossible for a New Testament believer to emulate, as it was focused on the sacrifice of animals and the worship of God in one location—the tabernacle or temple, depending on the time period. So this Old Testament story is once again a prophetic prototype of what we are to become.

AN OVERFLOW
OF WORSHIP

We are first and foremost a people of God's presence. The Church is the eternal dwelling place of God. As such we are known for our ministry *to God*, which positions and equips us for more effective ministry *to people*.

For example, evangelism in its purest form is simply an overflow of worship. If the glory of God could be seen on and within the house(s) of God in the Old Testament—though the hands of man built them—how much more is that glory witnessed in this house called the church; for God is building His Church (see Matt. 16:18).

HIS ETERNAL
DWELLING PLACE

We now have the privilege of ministering to God as they did in David's tabernacle. And the beautiful thing for us all is that this worship can and must be done in our homes, our cars, as well as in the corporate gatherings with our brothers and sisters.

Such a role has such a dramatic effect on the atmosphere here on earth that people become converted. My thinking is that the atmosphere in our homes and churches becomes so saturated with the glory of God in response to our worship that people are able to see and hear truth clearly.

Worship clears the airwaves. In that sense the Tabernacle of David, and its corresponding role in worship, is unchanged from the Old Testament to the New. Further study will again verify that the ministry of thanksgiving, praise, and worship—all aspects of our ministry unto Him—are all unchanged by the cross. In fact, it was the cross that brought this prototype out of the laboratory of an Old Testament experiment into the daily life of God's people, who have become His eternal dwelling place. It has become a norm.

Sing, O daughter of Zion!
Shout, O Israel!
Be glad and rejoice with all your heart,
O daughter of Jerusalem!
The Lord has taken away your judgments,
He has cast out your enemy.
The King of Israel, the Lord, is in your midst;
You shall see disaster no more.

In that day it shall be said to Jerusalem:
"Do not fear;
Zion, let not your hands be weak.
The Lord your God in your midst,
The Mighty One, will save;
He will rejoice over you with gladness,
He will quiet you with His love,
He will rejoice over you with singing."

—Zephaniah 3:14-17

About

BILL & BENI JOHNSON

Beni and Bill Johnson are the Senior Pastors of Bethel Church in Redding, California, and serve a growing number of churches that cross denominational lines. They are both bestselling authors, Bill, of *When Heaven Invades Earth* and *Hosting the Presence*, and Beni of *The Happy Intercessor*. They have three children and ten grandchildren.